40
BRIGHT & BOLD
PAPER-PIECED BLOCKS

12-INCH DESIGNS FROM CAROL DOAK

Martingale™
& COMPANY

Dedication

This book is dedicated to my brothers, Edwin Neal Carlson and John Theodore Carlson,
for their love, support, and friendship through the years.

Acknowledgments

My heartfelt thank-you and appreciation are extended to:
Ellen Peters, for her beautiful machine quilting;
Sherry Reis, for her friendship that is so dear and for offering to piece
the "Seaside" quilt and make the "Lighted Forest" quilt;
Timeless Treasures Fabrics, Inc., for the beautiful batik fabrics
used in the "Lighted Forest" quilt;
Ursula Reikes, for her friendship, fun, and for making what I do such a pleasure;
Everyone at Martingale & Company, for their support, friendship, and
all that they do to create my bright and bold books.

Credits

President . . . . Nancy J. Martin
CEO . . . . Daniel J. Martin
Publisher . . . . Jane Hamada
Editorial Director . . . . Mary V. Green
Managing Editor . . . . Tina Cook
Technical Editor . . . . Ursula Reikes
Copy Editor . . . . Liz McGehee
Design Director . . . . Stan Green
Illustrator . . . . Laurel Strand
Cover Designer . . . . Trina Stahl
Text Designer . . . . Regina Girard
Photographer . . . . Brent Kane

That Patchwork Place® is an imprint
of Martingale & Company™.

40 Bright and Bold Paper-Pieced Blocks:
12-Inch Designs from Carol Doak
© 2002 by Carol Doak

Martingale & Company
20205 144th Avenue NE
Woodinville, WA 98072-8478 USA
www.martingale-pub.com

Printed in the USA
07 06 05 04 03 02   8 7 6 5 4 3 2 1

Mission Statement

We are dedicated to providing quality products
and service by working together to inspire
creativity and to enrich the lives we touch.

Library of Congress Cataloging-in-Publication Data
Doak, Carol
    40 bright and bold paper-pieced blocks : 12-inch designs from Carol Doak.
        p. cm.
    ISBN 1-56477-394-9
    1. Patchwork—Patterns. 2. Machine quilting.
3. Patchwork quilts. I. Title: Forty bright and bold paper-pieced blocks. II. Title.

TT835 .D17 2002
746.46'041—dc21
                                    2001057955

CONTENTS

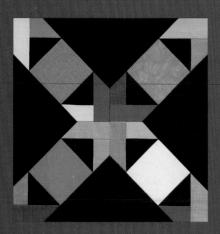

INTRODUCTION

Paper foundation piecing is such a wonderful method for creating accurate patchwork, even for beginning quilters! It never ceases to amaze me how the desire to use this easy patchwork method inspires exciting and creative patchwork possibilities, and how one idea often leads to another. After writing *50 Fabulous Paper-Pieced Stars*, which uses paper-pieced triangle sections to create 12" star blocks, I turned my thoughts to creating more 12" paper-pieced blocks, but with fewer pieces so they could be made quickly.

Whenever I begin designing a new series of block designs, I like to establish a set of guidelines to create a patchwork recipe that I can follow. For the blocks in this book, I came up with four guidelines. The first was to use four 6" block units in a four-block combination to make a 12" block. I decided on 6" block units because that size is easy to handle when paper piecing.

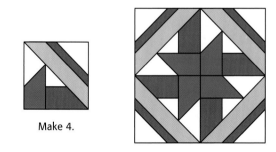

Make 4.

The second was to use a limited number of pieces to make each 6" unit so that the 12" blocks would be quick and easy to make. The pieces in each section range from 7 pieces to 16 pieces for a total of 28 to 64 pieces per 12" block.

The third was to create block designs that would work well as a single block and, in the case of some designs, would also make dramatic secondary patterns when used in a quilt.

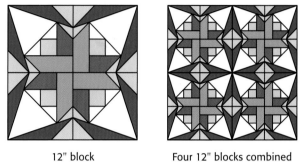

12" block   Four 12" blocks combined

The fourth was to create block designs using larger patchwork shapes so that fabric could be used in a way that would make bold statements.

With my patchwork recipe established, I started drafting the block designs. Very quickly, my thoughts turned to color and fabric possibilities for these new exciting designs. As I began to make my fabric selections and actually sew the blocks, it was fun to watch my blocks come to life. And this reminded me of the questions I often hear from workshop participants about how I select fabrics to make a dramatic statement. When I saw the results of my bold fabric choices, I knew I had to share these fabric-selection tips and tricks that I often rely upon.

Of course, the next obvious step was to make quilts using some of the blocks. In addition to the forty blocks, this book contains directions for eight quilts, which range in size from 36½" x 36½" to 72½" x 72½". These quilts are just a sampling of what you can make with these new blocks and easy fabric-cutting lists.

Now you can use accurate paper-piecing to make bold patchwork blocks and quilts quickly and easily.

All the best,

Carol

Using the right tools and supplies to create paper-pieced patchwork makes the process easy and fun. You will discover that the following items will do just that.

6" Add-a-Quarter ruler: This tool is invaluable for pretrimming the fabric pieces so you will know exactly where to place the next piece of fabric (see "Resources" on page 125).

Olfa rotary point cutter: Use this tool when you want to easily unsew a seam (see page 17).

Open-toe presser foot: This type of foot will allow you to easily see the needle go into the lines on the paper foundation.

Papers for Foundation Piecing: Use this lightweight paper when you copy the foundation piecing designs (see "Resources" on page 125).

Postcard: Use a sturdy postcard or 3" x 5" card to fold the paper foundation back on the next sewing line and trim the previously sewn fabric piece(s).

Rotary cutter and rotary mat: Choose a large rotary cutter that will allow you to cut through several layers of fabric.

Rotary rulers: The 6" x 12" and 6" x 6" rotary rulers are helpful for cutting the fabric and trimming the blocks.

Sandpaper tabs: Place stick-on sandpaper tabs (available at your quilt shop) every 3" along the length and ½" from the edge of the rotary ruler. This will prevent the ruler from slipping on the paper when you trim.

Scotch-brand removable tape: This tape will be helpful if you need to repair a foundation or resew across a previously sewn line.

Sewing thread: Use a standard 50-weight sewing thread. Match the thread to the general color value

of the fabrics. In most cases, you can rely upon white, medium gray, and black thread.

Silk pins with small heads or flat-headed pins: Because you will be pinning your first piece and then placing a postcard on top of the pin, use pins with small or flat heads that won't get in your way.

Size 90/14 sewing-machine needles: This larger needle will help to perforate the paper, making it easy to remove later.

Small stick-on notes: Label your stacks of cut fabric pieces with these. They will keep you organized and save time.

Stapler and staple remover: Use a stapler to secure several foundations for trimming, and a staple remover to remove the staple after the foundations are trimmed.

Thread clippers: A pair of thread clippers with narrow blades will assist you in clipping threads from the top and bottom of the foundation at the same time (see page 17). See "Resources" on page 125 to obtain more information about this tool.

Tweezers: Use tweezers to remove small bits of paper left behind in the intersecting seams.

Paper Foundations and Block-Front Drawings

MAKING THE PAPER FOUNDATIONS

Each 12" block requires four paper copies of the 6" unit. One way to make these paper foundations is to photocopy the designs on a copy machine. Be sure to check the accuracy of the machine against the original, and make all your copies for each block or quilt on the same copy machine from the original design. For a nominal fee, most copy shops will remove the binding of this book and three-hole punch the pages or spiral bind it to make using it on a copy machine even easier.

A copy machine that has the capability to reduce or enlarge offers the opportunity to create the blocks in a variety of sizes. The following chart shows the result of reduction and enlargement percentages:

Percentage of Enlargement or Reduction	Each Section	Finished Block Size
133 percent	8"	16"
125 percent	7½"	15"
117 percent	7"	14"
108 percent	6½"	13"
100 percent (original size)	6"	12"
92 percent	5½"	11"
83 percent	5"	10"
75 percent	4½"	9"
67 percent	4"	8"
58 percent	3½"	7"
50 percent	3"	6"
33 percent	2"	4"

Another way to make the foundation copies is to use your PC to print them. I personally feel copy machines are more important than vacuum cleaners; however, many households don't have copy machines while they do have PCs. If you want to print the foundations from your PC, you may purchase a companion computer program for this book that will permit you to print these foundations, change their size, and print them shaded, along with a few other options. The program specifics and ordering information are provided on page 125.

The foundation-piecing paper should hold up during the sewing process and be easy to remove when the top is complete. If in doubt, test your paper by sewing through it with a size 90/14 needle and a stitch length of 18 to 20 stitches per inch. If it tears as you sew, it is not strong enough. If it doesn't tear easily when pulled after sewing, it is too strong. The paper does not need to be translucent. The light from your sewing machine is sufficient to see through the blank side of the paper to the lines on the other side. The Papers for Foundation Piecing work well for these projects (see "Resources" on page 125).

After you make the necessary copies of each block, cut the blocks ½" from the outside line. To do this quickly and easily, staple the center of four papers together. Use your rotary cutter to trim the stapled foundations ½" from the solid outside line. Remove the staple.

USING THE BLOCK-FRONT DRAWINGS FOR CREATIVE OPTIONS

The small drawing on the bottom of each foundation page shows how the finished 6" unit will appear when it is completed. The numbered foundations are the reverse image of the finished unit. The block-front drawings show how the 6" units were positioned to create the sample 12" block. How the 6" units are positioned can make a dramatic difference in the finished 12" blocks. Look at how the position of the units in BB16, Ginny's block, were changed to create a new 12" block. Notice the differences in the resulting quilt patterns.

Changing the position of the colors within a block can also create very different blocks. See how the different color position changed BB19, Jenny's block, and the quilts made with this block.

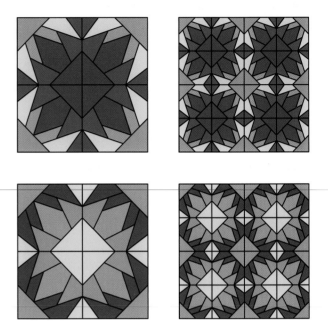

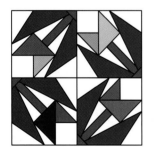

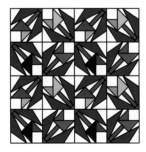

Original placement

Alternative placement

Changing the colors within a block can also produce interesting effects in a quilt design. The color placement in BB31, Rhoda's block, was changed in several blocks to produce a quilt design with a central focus.

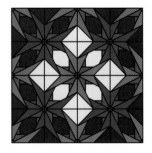

Make copies of the block-front drawings on the bottom of the foundation pages to experiment with unit and color placement.

BOLD FABRIC COMBINATIONS

Most quilters are passionate about their fabrics. Haven't you ever caressed a bolt of fabric that you fell in love with? However, when it is time to combine that fabric with other fabrics, many quilters become insecure about their choices. As I travel to lecture and teach, I am often asked about how I select a group of fabrics for a patchwork project.

Because many of the patchwork projects that I make are photographed and used in books or magazine articles, I often make bold fabric choices that photograph well. I rely upon a few simple concepts to make these bold selections.

COLOR INTENSITY

Color intensity is defined by the amount of gray in a color. A pure color has no gray to dull it. When choosing colors to make a bold statement, I look for pure colors with very little gray. In the following blocks, the fabrics used on the left are not pure colors, while the fabrics used on the right are. Can you see that the block on the right is much more dramatic and bold?

 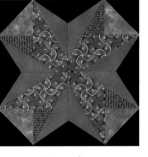

Grayed colors   Pure colors

HIGH CONTRAST

Another way to create a bold statement is to create high contrast in your block by combining very light and very dark fabrics. Adding just a touch of white or black fabric to your block can also create impact.

The addition of a bit of black in the following block makes it bolder.

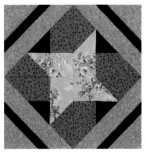

Black provides contrast

Even if a color in one of your fabrics happens to be a medium shade, you can add a much darker or lighter shade of that color to make a bolder statement. In the first block below, a medium-value floral fabric along with similar shades are used to make an OK block. However, the second block is much more dramatic because of the high contrast created by the darker pinks and greens.

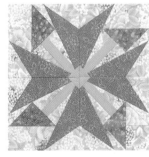 

Similar shades   Contrasting shades

WARM AND COOL COLORS

Warm colors are those that you would see in a fire, such as red, yellow, orange, and pink. Cool colors are shades of blue and green—colors you associate with the sky, water, and grass. Combining warm and cool colors in your patchwork helps to make a bold statement. Notice the blues and greens (both cool colors) used in the first block shown on page 10.

Then look at the shades of blue (a cool color) and yellow (a warm color) used in the second block. Can you see the dramatic difference that occurs when warm and cool colors are used together in the same block?

Cool colors Cool and warm colors

MAIN-PLAYER FABRICS

If you find it difficult to imagine how a combination of colors will work together, try choosing one fabric that contains a group of colors that you are passionate about. I call these main-player fabrics. Once you find a main-player fabric, it's easy to select other fabrics based on the colors in the main-player fabric. In the following blocks, main-player fabrics were used to help choose the other fabrics for the blocks.

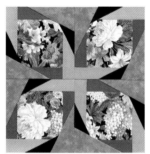

The blues, yellows, and greens in the background print inspired the other fabric choices.

The dynamic colors in this block were pulled from the floral print.

CREATING BOLD FABRIC OPTIONS

Keeping in mind the preceding fabric-selection tips, use the following options to create bold patchwork blocks.

- If you are at a loss for a combination of colors, choose a main-player fabric with several colors

that you like as the inspiration for the additional fabric colors.

- If the values of the colors you are selecting are similar, choose warm and cool colors to make them stand apart from each other.

- If the color in your main player is somewhat muted, choose clearer colors to make a more dramatic impact.

- If your color choices appear dull, add some high-contrast fabric values or a bit of white or black to create a high-impact detail.

- If your patchwork consists of all warm or cool colors, use clear colors or high contrast to make it bolder.

WORKING WITH GRAIN LINE AND DIRECTIONAL FABRIC

The good news is that foundation piecing means that you can ignore fabric grain for mechanical reasons, because the paper foundation supports the fabric so it will not stretch. However, fabric grain is important for visual reasons. In some cases, the same fabric will be placed along seam lines going in different directions, causing the grain of the fabric to go in different directions. Choose nondirectional print fabrics for background areas to avoid seeing the print go in several different directions. You may choose a directional print for one design element inside the unit because it will be consistent with the other three units. The following blocks illustrate this point.

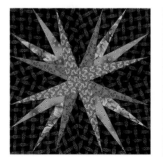

Directional fabric used in the background is distracting and not a good choice.

Nondirectional fabric used in the background is a good choice.

Paper-Piecing Techniques

MEASURING FABRIC-PIECE SIZE

There are cutting lists for each of the blocks in this book, and I feel they're worth their weight in gold! In the event you decide to enlarge or reduce these blocks, you will want to know how to measure for the correct-size fabric piece.

To measure for piece #1, place your ruler over piece #1 in the same way you intend to place your fabric. Look through the ruler to determine how large the piece needs to be, then add a generous seam allowance. I rely upon the approximate size, plus ¾" total for seam allowances.

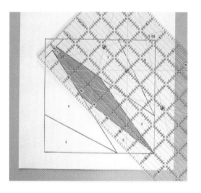

To measure subsequent pieces, place the ruler on the seam line you will sew next and let the ruler fall over the piece. This is how you will be placing your fabric so this is how you will measure. Look through the ruler to determine the needed size, plus a generous seam allowance.

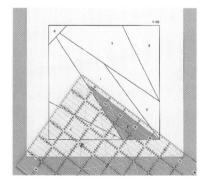

To measure for half-square triangles (straight grain on the short side of the triangle), measure the short side of the triangle and cut a square 1¼" larger. Cut this square once diagonally to make two half-square triangles.

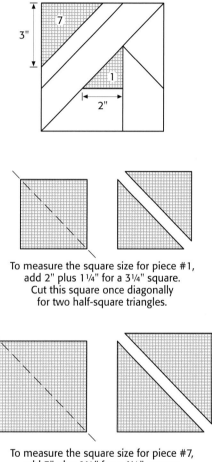

To measure the square size for piece #1, add 2" plus 1¼" for a 3¼" square. Cut this square once diagonally for two half-square triangles.

To measure the square size for piece #7, add 3" plus 1¼" for a 4¼" square. Cut this square once diagonally for two half-square triangles.

To measure quarter-square triangles (straight grain on the long side of the triangle), measure the long side of the triangle and cut a square 1½" larger. Cut this square twice diagonally to make four quarter-square triangles.

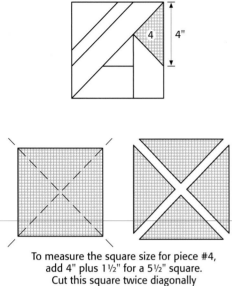

To measure the square size for piece #4, add 4" plus 1½" for a 5½" square. Cut this square twice diagonally for four quarter-square triangles.

CALCULATING YARDAGE FOR A PROJECT

If you would like to use these blocks to make a quilt, you can use a simple formula to calculate the yardage. The cutting list for each of the blocks provides the number and size of the pieces needed from each fabric to make one 12" block.

1. Establish how many 12" blocks you will make and multiply that number by the number of pieces for one 12" block to determine the number of pieces you need to cut. For example, if you are making nine of BB1, Allison's block, determine the number of pieces for the medium blue fabric (in the first line of the cutting list) by multiplying 9 (blocks) times 2 (number of pieces required for one block), or 18 pieces.

2. Each of these 18 pieces is 4¼" x 4¼". To determine how many 4¼" pieces you can cut from a full width of fabric, divide 42" (the width of the fabric) by 4¼" (the length of the piece), or 9.88. That means you can get 9 pieces from a 42"-long piece of fabric; you are not concerned with the fraction because you want full pieces, not partial pieces.

3. If you can get 9 pieces from a strip, then divide the total number of pieces needed (18) by the number you can cut from a strip (9) to determine how many strips you need to cut. The answer is 2 (18 divided by 9).

4. Now that you know you need to cut 2 strips, multiply the width of the strip times the number of strips needed. Since you are cutting a 4¼" square, the width of each of the 2 strips is 4¼" (2 times 4¼" equals 8½"). Therefore, you will need 8½" of fabric for these pieces.

5. If you need to cut other pieces from this same fabric, follow the same formula and add the yardage. When purchasing fabrics from calculated yardage, add a bit extra for shrinkage and for straightening the fabric.

So to recap, the formula for figuring yardage is as follows:

1. Determine the number of pieces needed by multiplying the number of pieces in the cutting list for one 12" block times the number of blocks you are making.

2. Determine how many pieces you can cut from a strip by dividing the width of your fabric (42") by the length of the piece or use the chart on page 13.

3. Determine the number of strips to cut by dividing the number of pieces needed by the number that you can cut from a strip.

4. Determine the fabric yardage for those pieces by multiplying the number of strips to cut by the width of the piece.

SPEED CUTTING

When making quilts, I look for the most efficient way to accomplish the task. When I was making the quilts for this book, I discovered that I could significantly reduce the amount of time I spent cutting out the fabric pieces by using the following method.

First, determine how many pieces can be cut from a 42"-wide strip by dividing the length of the piece to cut by 42" (the full width of the fabric).

The following chart lists calculations for several different lengths, up to 7¼".

Cut pieces from a 42"-wide strip.	
Cut Lengths	**Number of Pieces**
1"	42
1¼"	33
1½"	28
1¾"	24
2"	21
2¼"	18
2½"	16
2¾"	15
3"	14
3¼"	12
3½"	12
3¾"	11
4"	10
4¼"	9
4½"	9
4¾"	8
5"	8
5¼"	8
5½"	7
6"	7
6¼"	6
6½"	6
7"	6
7¼"	5

Second, divide the total number of pieces needed (found in the cutting lists) by the number you can cut from a strip to determine how many strips to cut. For instance, if you need to cut 100 pieces, each 2" x 3", refer to the chart and notice that you can cut 14 pieces, each 3" long, from 1 strip. Since you need 100 pieces, divide 100 pieces by 14 pieces to determine the number of 2"-wide strips to cut (7.14); this number indicates that you need to cut 7 strips and a bit of another. Therefore, you would cut 8 strips, each 2" wide, into one-hundred 2" x 3" pieces.

You can place several strips, folded in half, on top of each other to cut multiple layers at one time. I found that cutting four folded strips (or eight layers) is fine. When more than four strips are involved, align the subsequent layered strips along the long edge of the first group of strips. Since you only need to cut a few pieces from the eighth strip in the example, don't include it in this layered group and cut those additional pieces separately.

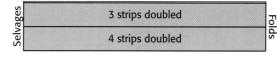
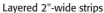

Layered 2"-wide strips

Remove the selvage edges and cut the 3"-long pieces. Keep track of the total number of pieces you cut as you cut them.

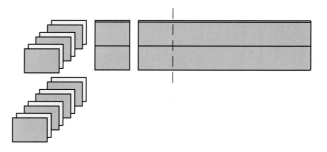

Label the stack of fabrics with the location numbers listed in the cutting list.

13

STEP-BY-STEP PAPER PIECING

Up to this point, you should have selected the block you want, made copies of your foundation, cut your fabric pieces, and labeled them. So gather your sewing supplies, because you are ready to paper-foundation piece. We'll use a section from BB1, Allison's block (page 22), as an example.

1. Use a size 90/14 sewing-machine needle, an open-toe presser foot for good visibility, and a stitch length of 18 to 20 stitches per inch. This is approximately 1.5 on a sewing machine that has a stitch-length range of 0 to 5. The larger needle and smaller stitch length will allow you to remove the paper easily.

2. Using the light on your sewing machine, look through the blank side of the paper to place piece #1 right side up over the area marked #1. Turn the paper over and make sure it covers area #1 and extends at least ¼" beyond all seam lines. Pin in place. Place the pin parallel to the seam line between areas #1 and #2.

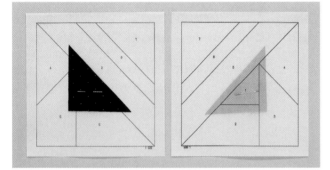

3. Place the postcard on the line between areas #1 and #2, and fold the paper back to expose the excess fabric beyond the seam line.

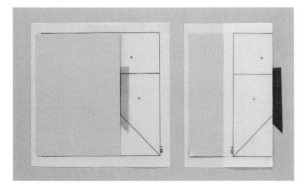

4. Place the Add-a-Quarter ruler on the fold and trim the excess fabric ¼" from the fold. The lip on the ruler prevents it from slipping as you trim. Or you can align the ¼" line on a rotary ruler with the fold to trim.

5. Looking through the blank side of the paper to the design on the other side, place piece #2 right side up over area #2. This is an important step. The reason you want to look through the blank side of the paper to position the next piece of fabric is to see how the fabric will appear after it is sewn and pressed open. Remember, what you see is what you get.

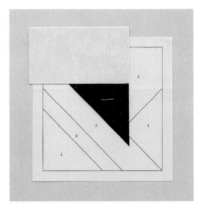

After piece #2 is properly positioned, flip it right sides together with the just-trimmed edge of piece #1. Looking through the blank side of the paper again, check that the ends of piece #2 extend beyond the seam lines of area #2 on the foundation.

If you are using cotton fabric, piece #2 should cling to piece #1, but if it makes you more comfortable, you can pin piece #2 in place. If you are using slippery fabrics such as satins, definitely pin piece #2 in place.

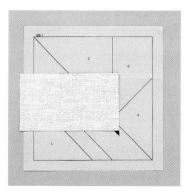

6. Place the foundation under the presser foot and sew on the seam line between areas #1 and #2, beginning about ¼" to ½" before the seam and extending the stitching about the same distance beyond the end of the seam.

7. Clip the threads (see tip on page 17). Remove the pin and open piece #2. If you are using cotton fabrics, press with a dry iron on the cotton setting. If you are using heat-sensitive fabrics, use a pressing cloth or lower the temperature

on the iron. Cover your ironing surface with a piece of scrap fabric to protect it from any ink that may transfer from the photocopies.

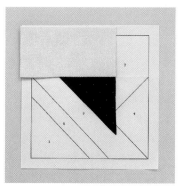

8. Place the postcard on the next line you will sew. This is where piece #3 adjoins the previous pieces. Fold the paper back, exposing the excess fabrics. With this seam, it will be necessary to pull the stitches away from the foundation to fold the paper. Place the Add-a-Quarter ruler on the fold and trim ¼" from the fold.

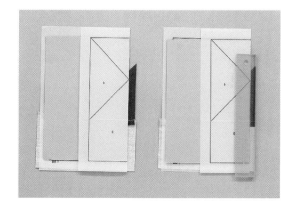

9. Place piece #3 right side up over area #3 to check for proper placement. Place the fabric right sides together with the just-trimmed edges of pieces #1 and #2. See how the fabric

extends on both sides for adequate seam allowances? Sew and press open.

10. Continue with piece #4 by placing the postcard on the line between areas #3 and #4. Fold the paper back and trim the excess fabric ¼" from the fold. Place piece #4 right side up over area #4 to check for proper placement; then flip it right sides together along the just-trimmed edge. Sew and press open.

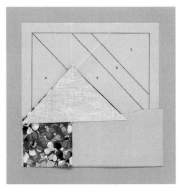

11. Continue in the same manner until piece #6 has been added and trimmed. Place piece #7 right side up and then flip it right sides together with piece #6. Check that piece #7 is centered by aligning the center point on the fabric triangle with the center point of the triangle on the

foundation paper. Sew the seam and press the piece open.

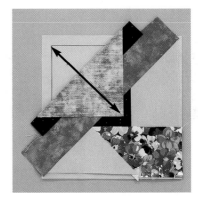

12. Using the rotary ruler, align the ¼" line on the outside sewing line and trim the foundation ¼" from the sewing line on all sides. Do not remove the paper yet.

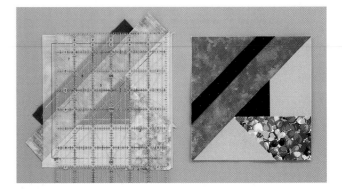

PAPER-PIECING TIPS

The following tips should help make your paper piecing a breeze.

• Set up a pressing area next to your sewing machine. You can even lower an ironing board to make a convenient area to press. Cover your ironing surface with a piece of scrap fabric since some of the ink from the copies may transfer when pressing.

- Use a small travel iron set on the cotton setting. If you are using heat-sensitive fabrics, adjust the iron temperature accordingly.

- Assembly-line sew like blocks without cutting the threads in between. This will speed up the paper-piecing process.

- I was shown a neat trick by one of my students that saves me lots of time clipping threads. With the paper side facing up, pull up on the top thread and it will pull the bobbin thread up slightly. In the photo, I used a black bobbin thread so you can see the loop that comes up when you pull on the top thread. Using sharp, curved, thin-blade thread clippers, clip close to the surface of the foundation; most times you will be able to cut the bobbin thread at the same time you are cutting the top threads. Give it a try and you may find that it saves you time, too.

- If it is necessary to repair a torn foundation, use Scotch-brand removable tape. Do not touch the iron directly to the tape.

- If it is necessary to remove a line of stitching, place a piece of Scotch-brand removable tape on the stitching line you need to remove. Pull the top fabric piece back to expose the thread.

Lightly touch the point of the Olfa rotary point cutter to the threads, keeping tension on the fabric as the threads are cut. This method of removing the stitches not only goes quickly, but the tape provides a good foundation for resewing the seam line.

- If you should unknowingly run out of bobbin thread while sewing and need to restitch the same line, use the tape along the seam line so the foundation will not tear when sewn again.

ADDING PIECED UNITS

Some paper-pieced designs have pieced units. When a pieced unit is indicated, one number is assigned to the unit and two slashes (//) are placed on the seam(s) that need to be pieced before adding the unit to the foundation. The pieced units are made up of fabric pieces that you sew together before adding them to the foundation. Pieced units may have one or two seams.

In BB16, Ginny's block, pieced unit 6 is the stem portion of the block. To make this piece, sew the strips together as indicated and crosscut them at the intervals indicated.

Position unit 6 and pin in place so it will not move when you are sewing the seam. Press unit 6 open and machine baste it in position near the base of the unit so it will not move when you add the subsequent pieces. Remove the basting when the block is complete.

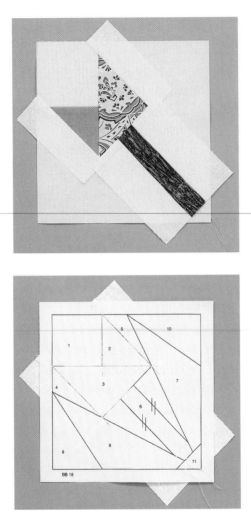

baste the beginning of the unit, the middle or any matching points along the seam, and the end of the unit. Check that you have a good match. If you would like to adjust the seam at any basting point, simply clip the basting threads and pull the thread from the bobbin side to remove it. Adjust and machine baste again. This basting technique not only gives you the opportunity to check for accuracy before you actually sew the seam, but it also prevents the foundations from slipping as you sew.

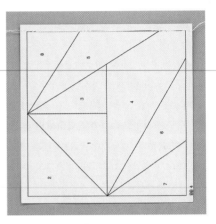

Once the top half is basted and sewn, press with the seam allowances to the left. Repeat this process with the bottom two units, pressing the seam so it will be going in the opposite direction from the seam in the top two units.

Repeat this process, joining the top half and bottom half of the blocks. Arrange the blocks in rows to determine which way to press the horizontal seam allowances so they oppose each other from block to block.

Do not remove the paper from the blocks until the blocks have been joined to other blocks or fabric pieces.

COMPLETING THE BLOCK

When the four units have been completed and trimmed, place them as indicated in the photograph or the block-front drawing. Place the top two units right sides together and pin the seam. Machine

18

BRIGHT AND BOLD BLOCKS

"Gallery of Blocks" on pages 20 and 21 presents all the blocks together. Use these pages to consider which blocks you would like to make.

As I worked on the block designs, I thought about how I should name them. I decided to name the blocks for many of the women at Martingale & Company along with some friends as a tribute to their involvement in the publishing of my books over the past ten years. And as in my previous books, I've also assigned numbers to each of the blocks to help keep them organized. For example, "BB16" is the numeric label for Ginny's block. The *BB* stands for Bright and Bold.

Following the gallery are photographs, fabric cutting lists, and foundations for forty blocks. Each block is pictured individually as well as in a four-block rotation to show how the blocks will appear when joined in a quilt.

All of the blocks are easy to make; however, your time investment will vary with the number of pieces required to make each block. The blocks have been arranged in alphabetical order, beginning with those with the fewest number of pieces and progressing to those with the most pieces.

The fabric-cutting lists provided with each block will make one 12" block. If you use similar fabric placement, simply substitute your color choices. If you decide to use a different fabric placement, check the size to cut for the appropriate location in the block and cut your pieces accordingly.

The ◺ symbol in the cutting list indicates to cut the squares once diagonally to create two half-square triangles (see page 11). The ⊠ symbol in the cutting list indicates to cut the squares twice diagonally to create four quarter-square triangles (see pages 11 and 12).

The foundation pages include full-size paper-piecing foundations for each block unit. The foundations are the reverse of the finished unit because you will be sewing from the back of the design.

Make four 6" units to create one 12" block. Arrange the completed units as indicated in the block-front drawings or as desired. Remember, the units can be placed in a different rotation, resulting in a different design (see page 8).

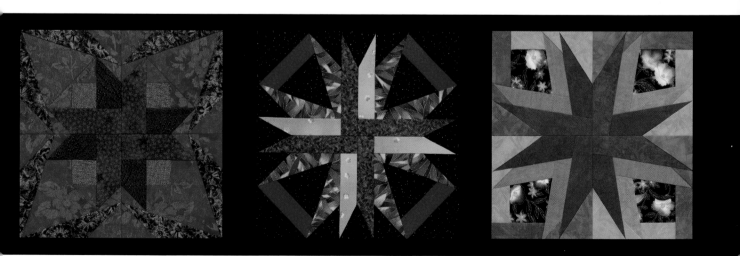

GALLERY OF BLOCKS

Page 22

Page 24

Page 26

Page 28

Page 30

Page 32

Page 34

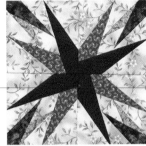

Page 36

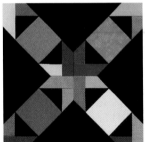

Page 37

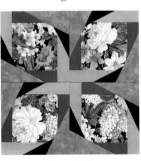

Page 40

Page 42

Page 44

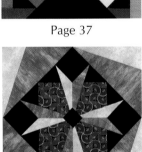

Page 46

Page 48

Page 50

Page 52

Page 54

Page 56

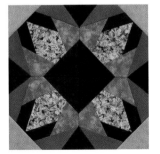

Page 58

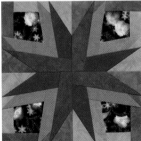

Page 60

Page 62

Page 64

Page 66

Page 68

Page 70

Page 72

Page 74

Page 76

Page 78

Page 80

Page 82

Page 84

Page 86

Page 88

Page 90

Page 92

Page 94

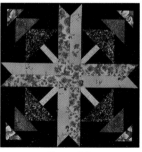

Page 96

Page 98

Page 100

ALLISON'S BLOCK

28 PIECES

The following cutting list is for one 12" block.

Fabric	No. of Pieces	Dimensions	Location Numbers
Medium blue	2	4¼" x 4¼" ◻	7
	4	2" x 9½"	5
Dark blue	1	5½" x 5½" ⊠	4
	4	2¾" x 5"	2
Black	2	3¼" x 3¼" ◻	1
	4	1½" x 7"	6
Yellow	4	2¾" x 5"	3

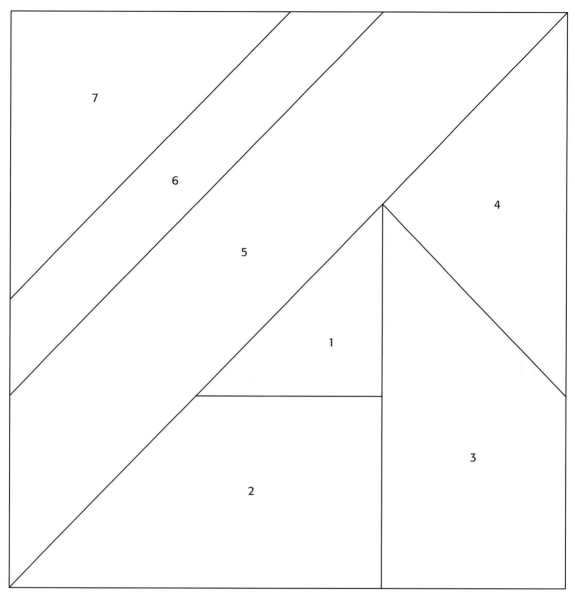

BB1: Allison's Block

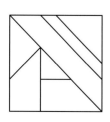

Make 4.

Block-Front Drawings

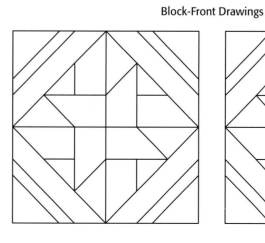

BARBARA'S BLOCK

28 Pieces

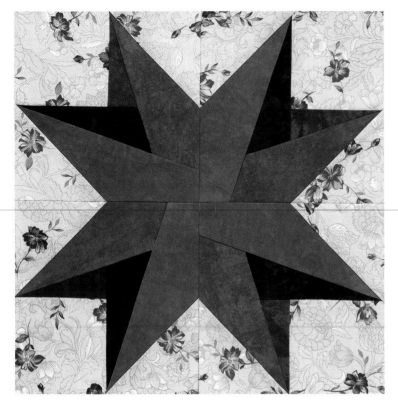

The following cutting list is for one 12" block.

Fabric	No. of Pieces	Dimensions	Location Numbers
Light purple floral	4	4¼" x 4¼" ◻	6, 7
	4	3¾" x 3¾"	1
Dark green	4	2¼" x 5½"	3
Medium green	4	1¾" x 3¾"	2
Fuchsia	4	2½" x 6½"	4
Medium purple	4	2½" x 7½"	5

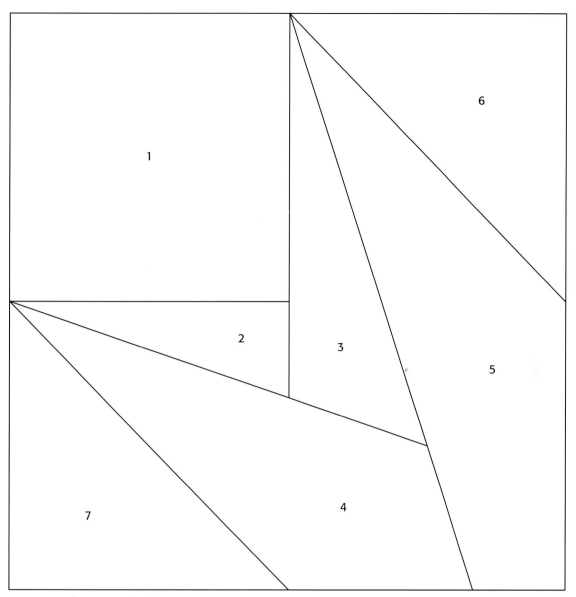

BB2: Barbara's Block

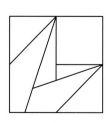

Make 4.

Block-Front Drawings

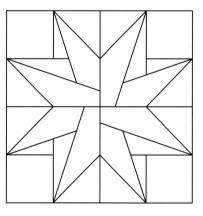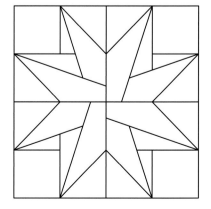

BETH'S BLOCK

32 Pieces

The following cutting list is for one 12" block.

Fabric	No. of Pieces	Dimensions	Location Numbers
Black print	8	2½" x 6"	6, 7
	8	2" x 6"	2, 3
Floral print	8	3" x 7½"	4, 5
Red	4	2¼" x 9"	1
Green	2	2¼" x 2¼" ◫	8

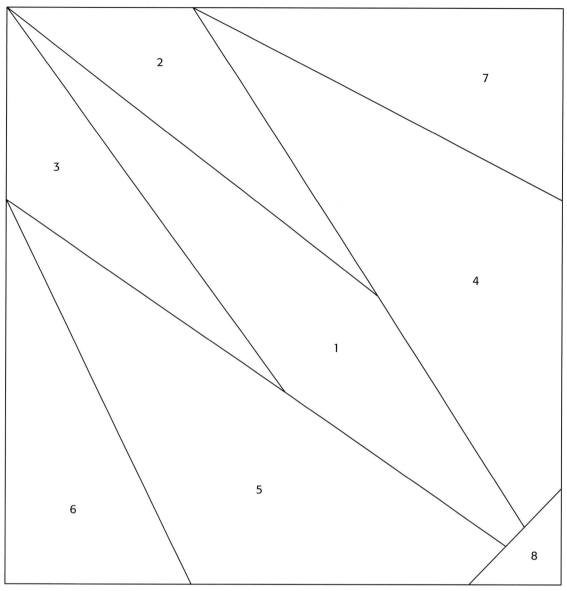

BB3: Beth's Block

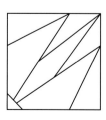

Make 4.

Block-Front Drawings

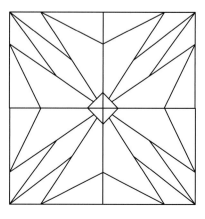 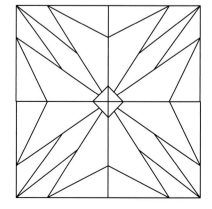

BONNIE'S BLOCK

32 PIECES

The following cutting list is for one 12" block.

Fabric	No. of Pieces	Dimensions	Location Numbers
White print	2	4¼" x 4¼" ◻	1
	8	2½" x 5"	7, 8
Medium fuchsia	8	2¼" x 7"	5, 6
Dark fuchsia	2	4¼" x 4¼" ◻	2
Yellow	4	2½" x 4"	3
Dark blue	4	3¾" x 7"	4

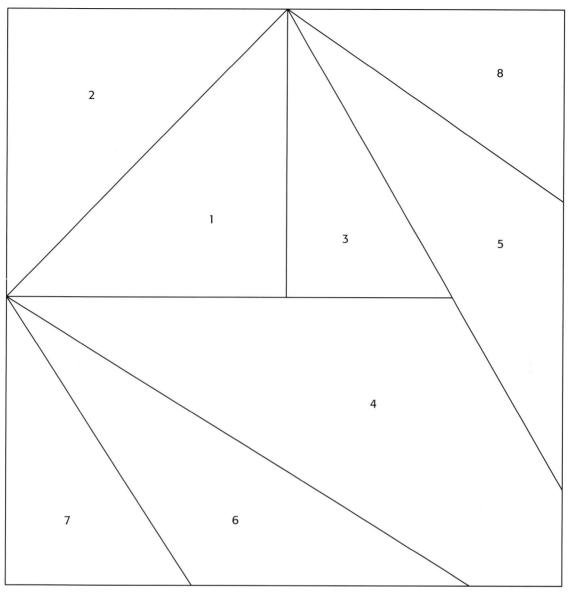

BB4: Bonnie's Block

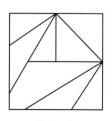

Make 4.

Block-Front Drawings

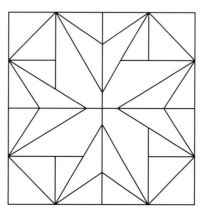 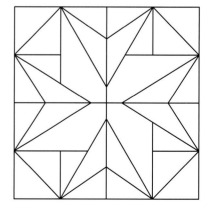

Carol's Block

32 Pieces

The following cutting list is for one 12" block.

Fabric	No. of Pieces	Dimensions	Location Numbers
Light blue	6	4¼" x 4¼" ⧅	2, 7, 8
White	2	4¼" x 4¼" ⧅	1
Medium blue	4	2¼" x 3¾"	3
Dark blue	4	2¼" x 5¼"	6
Medium yellow	4	2¼" x 3¾"	4
Dark yellow	4	2¼" x 5¼"	5

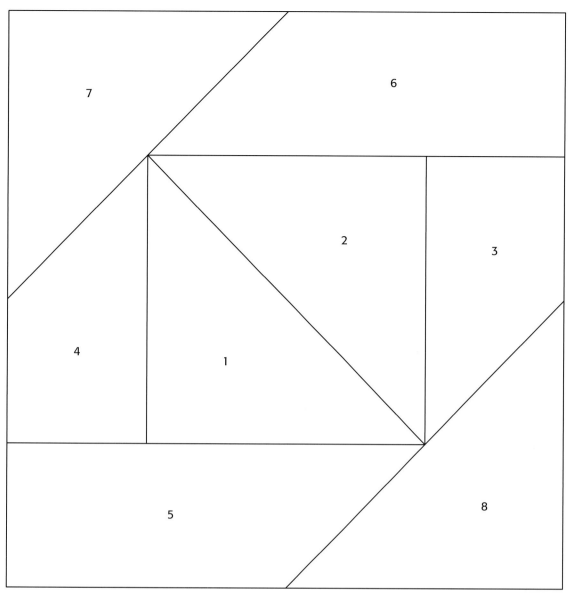

BB5: Carol's Block

Block-Front Drawings

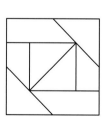

Make 4.

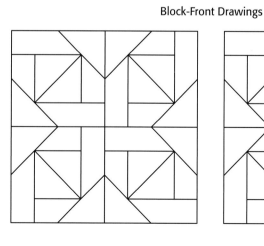

CAROLYN'S BLOCK

32 PIECES

The following cutting list is for one 12" block.

Fabric	No. of Pieces	Dimensions	Location Numbers
Black	4	3¼" x 3¼" ◱	1, 7
	4	2¾" x 4¾"	5
Black and gold	2	3¼" x 3¼" ◳	8
Black-and-beige paisley	4	2¾" x 6¾"	6
Beige check	2	5¼" x 5¼" ◳	4
Beige	4	1¾" x 4¾"	3
	4	1¾" x 3¾"	2

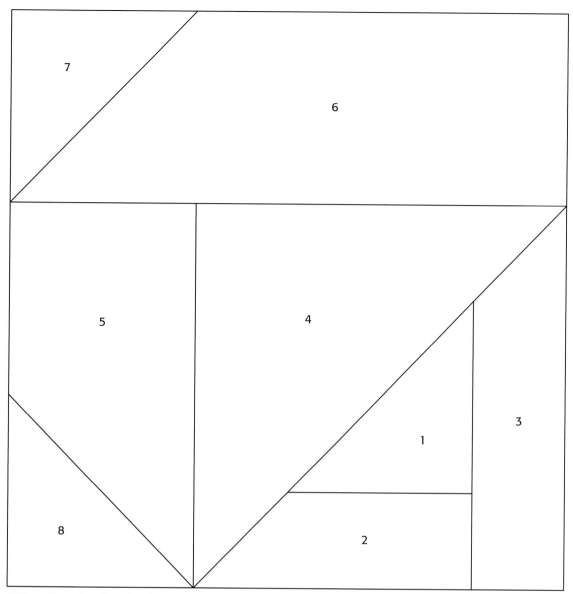

BB6: Carolyn's Block

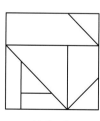

Make 4.

Block-Front Drawings

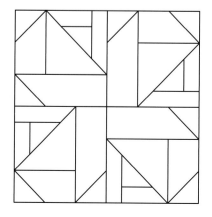

CHRIS'S BLOCK

36 PIECES

 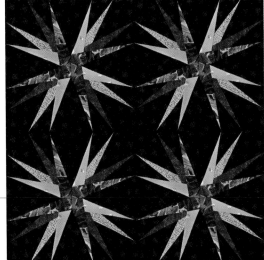

The following cutting list is for one 12" block.

Fabric	No. of Pieces	Dimensions	Location Numbers
Black	4	3½" x 6½"	1
	8	2½" x 6½"	8, 9
	8	2½" x 5"	4, 5
Green #1	4	1½" x 6½"	2
Green #2	4	1½" x 6½"	3
Green #3	4	1¾" x 6½"	6
Green #4	4	1¾" x 7"	7

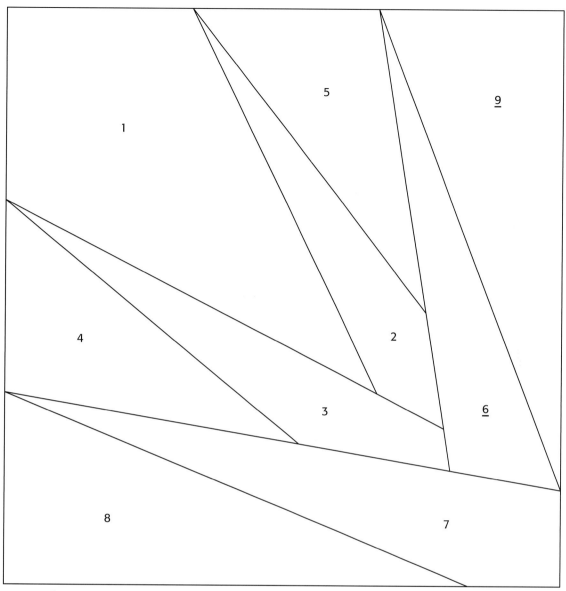

BB7: Chris's Block

Block-Front Drawings

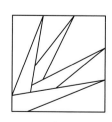

Make 4.

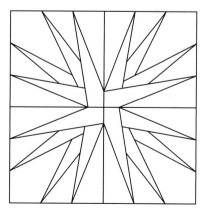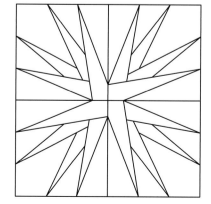

CINDI'S BLOCK

36 PIECES

The following cutting list is for one 12" block.

Fabric	No. of Pieces	Dimensions	Location Numbers
Light green	8	3" x 6"	8, 9
	8	2" x 5½"	4, 5
	4	2" x 4"	1
Medium green	4	2" x 5"	2
Dark green	4	2" x 6"	3
Medium blue	4	2¼" x 6½"	6
Dark blue	4	2¼" x 8"	7

BB8: Cindi's Block

Block-Front Drawings

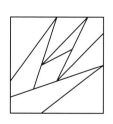

Make 4.

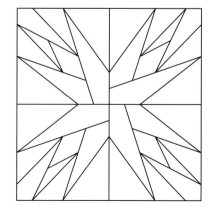

CLAUDIA'S BLOCK

36 PIECES

The following cutting list is for one 12" block.

Fabric	No. of Pieces	Dimensions	Location Numbers
Black	4	5¼" x 5¼" ◻	8, 9
	4	3¼" x 3¼" ◻	2, 3
Assorted solid colors	4	3½" x 3½"	1
	8	1¾" x 4"	6, 7
	8	1¾" x 3"	4, 5

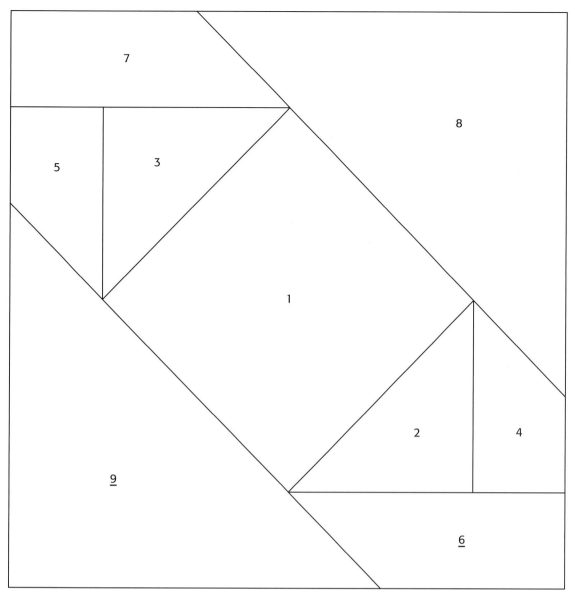

BB9: Claudia's Block

Block-Front Drawings

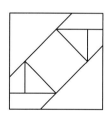

Make 4.

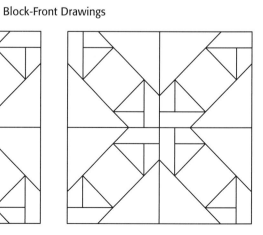

CLEO'S BLOCK

36 PIECES

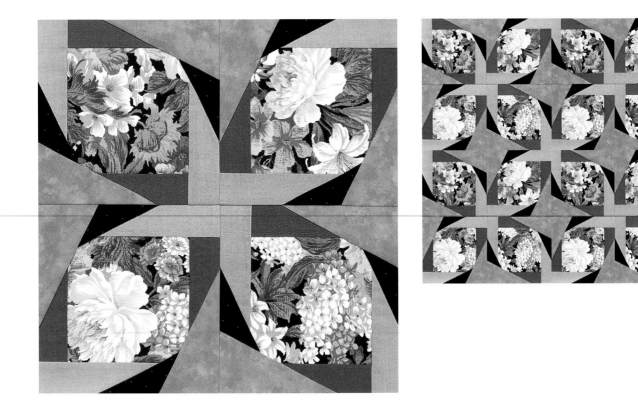

The following cutting list is for one 12" block.

Fabric	No. of Pieces	Dimensions	Location Numbers
Floral	4	4¾" x 4¾"	1
Medium pink	8	1¾" x 3¾"	2, 3
Light pink	8	1¾" x 4¾"	4, 5
Black	8	1½" x 4"	6, 7
Teal	8	2½" x 5¾"	8, 9

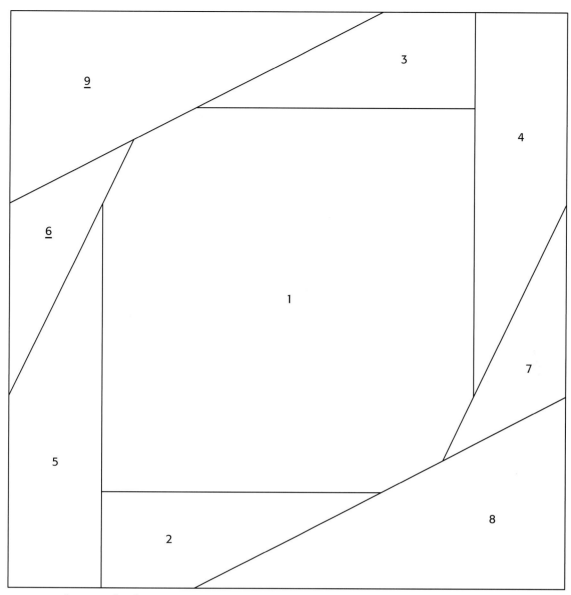

BB10: Cleo's Block

Block-Front Drawings

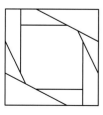

Make 4.

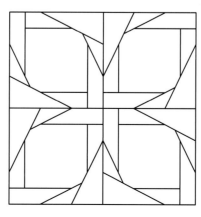

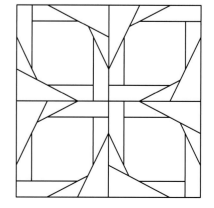

CORNELIA'S BLOCK

36 PIECES

The following cutting list is for one 12" block.

Fabric	No. of Pieces	Dimensions	Location Numbers
Floral print	4	4¼" x 4¼" ◺	7, 9
	8	2½" x 3¼"	2, 3
Blue	8	2¾" x 6"	4, 5
Rose	4	2½" x 4½"	1
Purple	2	4¼" x 4¼" ◺	8
Navy	2	4¼" x 4¼" ◺	6

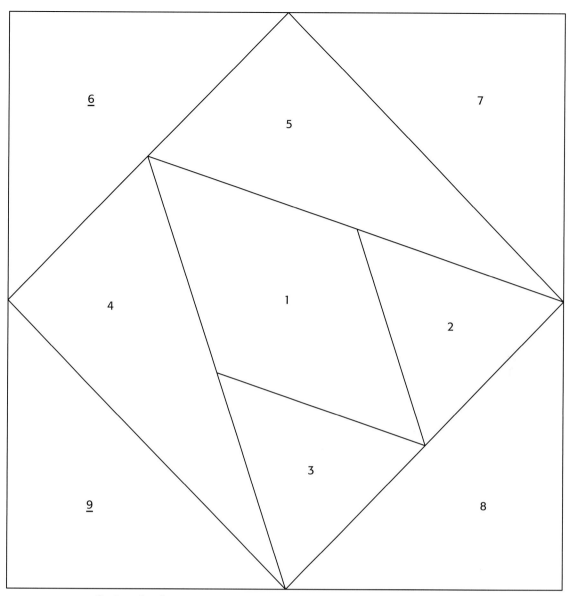

BB11: Cornelia's Block

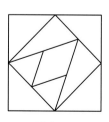

Make 4.

Block-Front Drawings

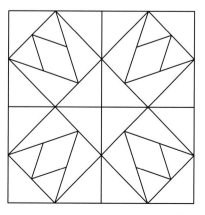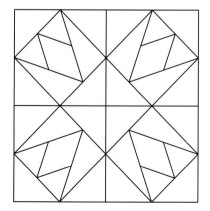

DAWN'S BLOCK

40 PIECES

 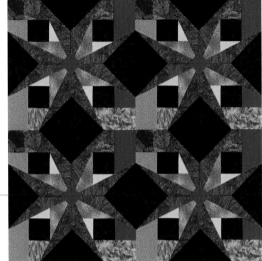

The following cutting list is for one 12" block.

Fabric	No. of Pieces	Dimensions	Location Numbers
Black	4	4¼" x 4¼" ◻	8 (A, B, C, D); 9 (A, B, C, D)
	4	2¾" x 2¾"	1 (A, B, C, D)
Yellow	4	1¾" x 3"	2 (A, B, C, D)
Orange	4	2½" x 5"	4 (A, B, C, D)
Green	8	2" x 7"	6 (A, B, C, D); 7 (A, B, C, D)
Dark orange	1	2¾" x 5"	5A
	1	2¾" x 2¾"	3B
Red	1	2¾" x 5"	5B
	1	2¾" x 2¾"	3C
	2	2¼" x 2¼" ◻	10 (A, B, C, D)
Gold	1	2¾" x 5"	5C
	1	2¾" x 2¾"	3D
Peach	1	2¾" x 5"	5D
	1	2¾" x 2¾"	3A

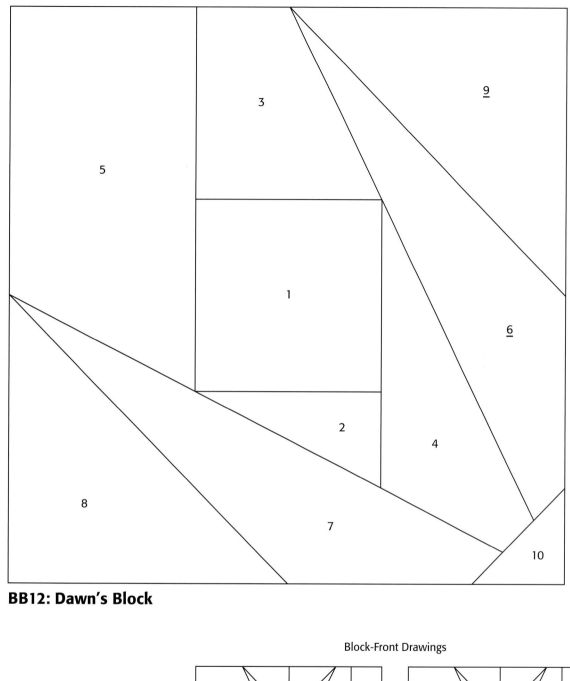

BB12: Dawn's Block

Block-Front Drawings

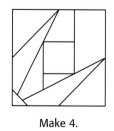

Make 4.

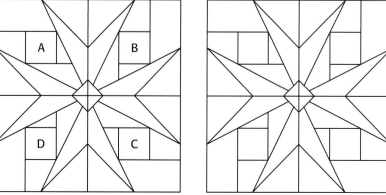

Note: The fabric placement is the same for all locations except for numbers 3 and 5, where it will change for each of the 4 blocks to create the woven effect. Label your foundations A, B, C, and D to place the fabrics correctly.

DONNA'S BLOCK

40 PIECES

The following cutting list is for one 12" block.

Fabric	No. of Pieces	Dimensions	Location Numbers
Black	2	4½" x 4½" ⊠	6, 7
	8	2¼" x 2¾"	2, 3
	2	2¼" x 2¼" ◲	8
Red-and-orange print	4	3½" x 4¼"	1
Yellow	4	2½" x 7½"	10
	4	1½" x 5"	4
Orange	4	3½" x 9½"	9
	4	1½" x 5"	5

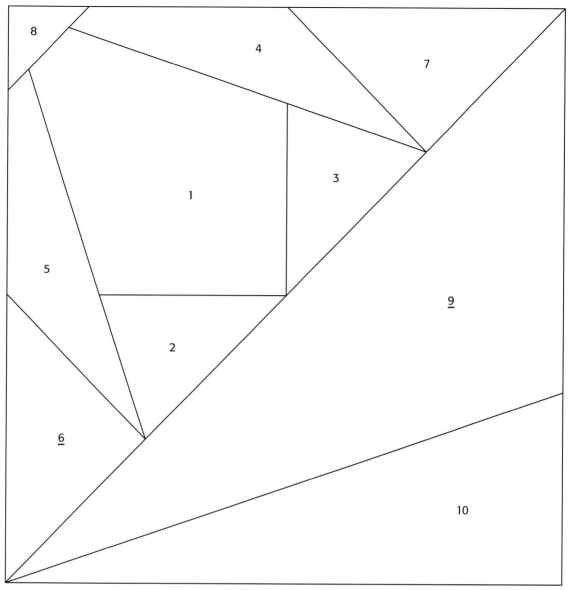

BB13: Donna's Block

Block-Front Drawings

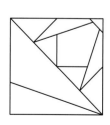

Make 4.

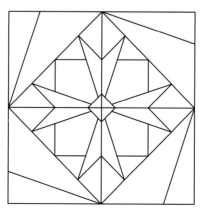

EILEEN'S BLOCK

44 PIECES

The following cutting list is for one 12" block.

Fabric	No. of Pieces	Dimensions	Location Numbers
Medium blue	16	2½" x 4½"	3, 4, 9, 10
	2	2¼" x 2¼" ◻	2
Yellow	4	2" x 4¼"	1
	2	2¼" x 2¼" ◻	11
Green #1	4	2¼" x 4"	5
Green #2	4	3½" x 6½"	6
Light blue #1	4	2½" x 7"	7
Light blue #2	4	2½" x 7"	8

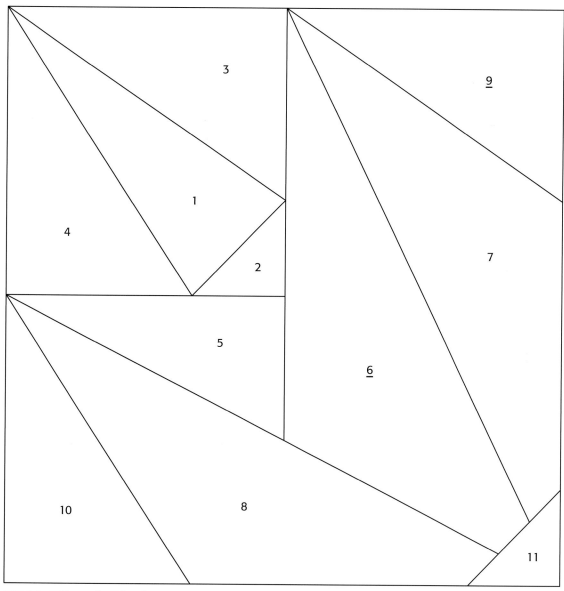

BB14: Eileen's Block

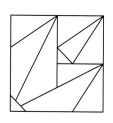

Make 4.

Block-Front Drawings

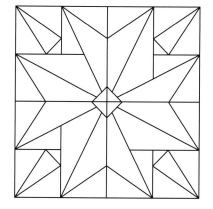

ELLEN'S BLOCK

44 PIECES

The following cutting list is for one 12" block.

Fabric	No. of Pieces	Dimensions	Location Numbers
Light pink	8	2¾" x 2¾" ◻	6, 7, 10, 11
	4	2" x 2"	1
Medium pink #1	4	2" x 5 1/2"	8
	4	1½" x 4½"	5
Medium pink #2	4	2" x 7"	9
	4	1½" x 4"	4
Dark pink #1	4	3¼" x 4½"	3
Dark pink #2	4	2" x 3¼"	2

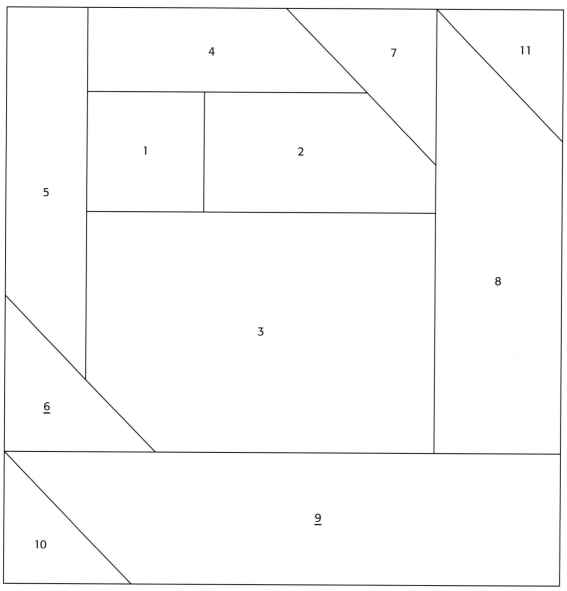

BB15: Ellen's Block

Block-Front Drawings

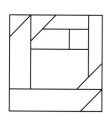

Make 4.

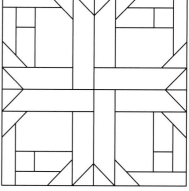

GINNY'S BLOCK
44 PIECES

The following cutting list is for one 12" block.

Fabric	No. of Pieces	Dimensions	Location Numbers
Floral print	4	2¾" x 2¾"	1
	8	2½" x 5"	9, 10
	2	1¾" x 18"	pieced unit 6*
	8	1½" x 4"	4, 5
Dark pink	1	5½" x 5½" ⊠	3
Medium pink	2	3¼" x 3¼" ◻	2
Dark green	2	2¼" x 2¼" ◻	11
	1	1¼" x 18"	pieced unit 6*
Medium green	8	2½" x 7"	7, 8

*To make pieced unit 6, sew the floral-print strips on the long sides of the dark green strip. Press the seam allowances toward the middle. Crosscut 4 pieces, each 4¼" wide. Pin pieced unit in place, sew, and press open. Machine baste at loose end so it will not move when you add the subsequent pieces (see page 18).

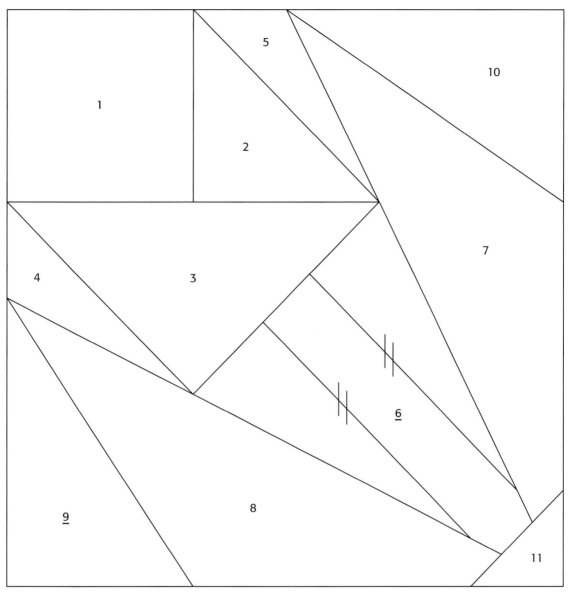

BB16: Ginny's Block

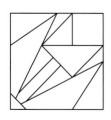

Make 4.

Block-Front Drawings

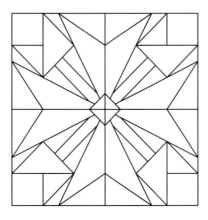

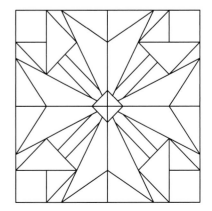

JANE'S BLOCK

44 PIECES

The following cutting list is for one 12" block.

Fabric	No. of Pieces	Dimensions	Location Numbers
White	4	3¾" x 3¾"	1
	4	3¼" x 3¼" ◻	10, 11
	8	1¼" x 7"	6, 7
Floral print	4	2¾" x 4¾"	3
Purple	2	3¼" x 3¼" ◻	2
Green #1	4	1¾" x 3¾"	5
Green #2	4	1¾" x 2¾"	4
Yellow check	8	1¼" x 5¾"	8, 9

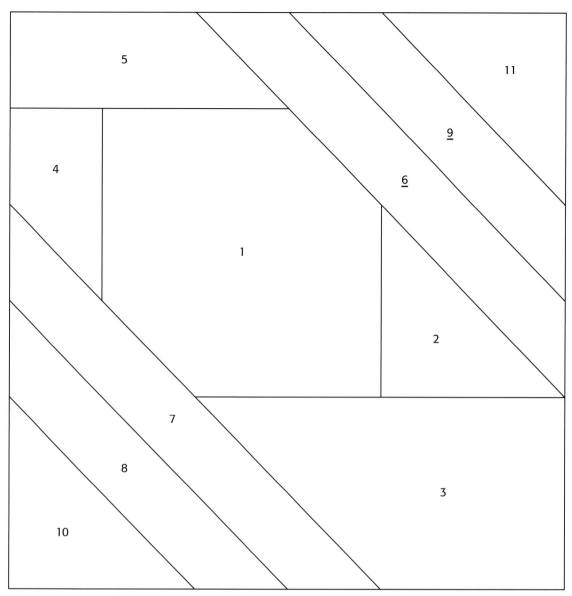

BB17: Jane's Block

Block-Front Drawings

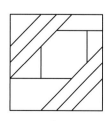

Make 4.

JANET'S BLOCK

44 PIECES

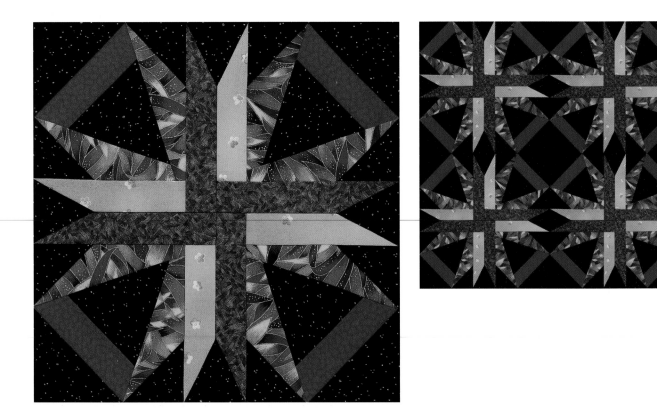

The following cutting list is for one 12" block.

Fabric	No. of Pieces	Dimensions	Location Numbers
Black	2	4¼" x 4¼" ◻	3
	4	4" x 4"	1
	4	3¼" x 3¼" ◻	6, 7
	8	1½" x 4"	10, 11
Red	4	1¾" x 5"	2
Floral print	8	2" x 6½"	4, 5
Light green	4	1¾" x 5¾"	8
Medium green	4	1¾" x 6¾"	9

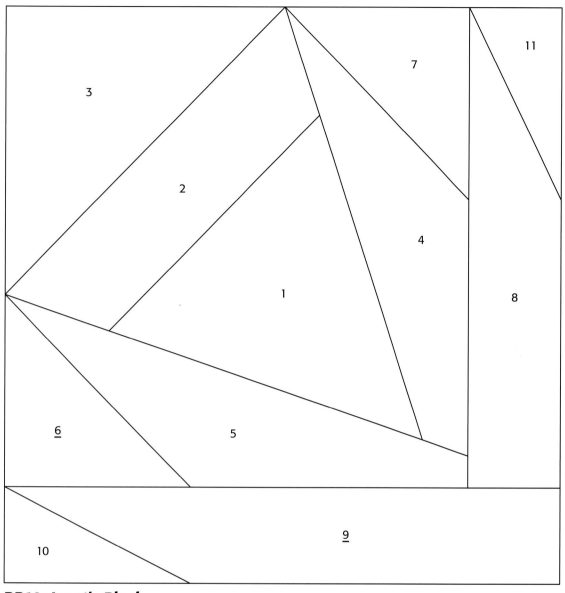

BB18: Janet's Block

Block-Front Drawings

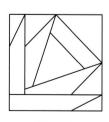

Make 4.

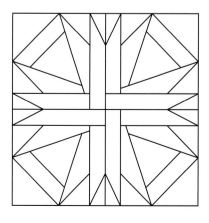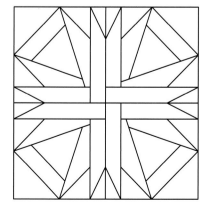

57

JENNY'S BLOCK

44 PIECES

 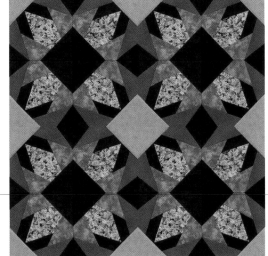

The following cutting list is for one 12" block.

Fabric	No. of Pieces	Dimensions	Location Numbers
Floral print	4	3¼" x 5"	1
Blue	8	2½" x 4"	4, 5
Purple	8	2" x 5"	6, 7
Green	2	4¼" x 4¼" ◻	10
Navy	2	4¼" x 4¼" ◻	11
	8	2" x 4"	8, 9
	8	1½" x 4"	2, 3

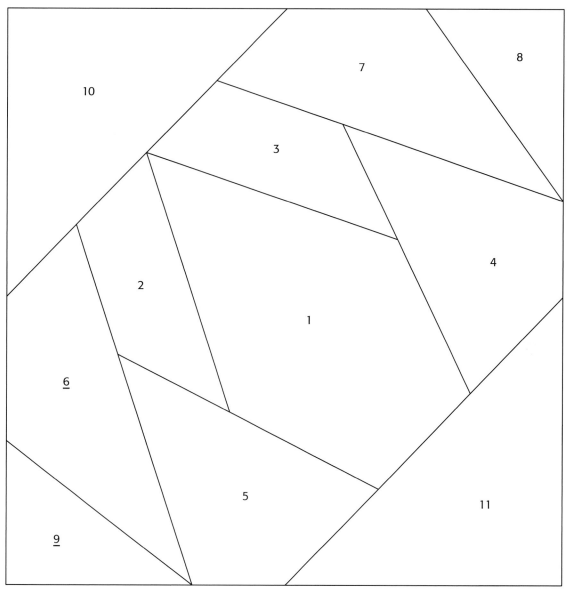

BB19: Jenny's Block

Block-Front Drawings

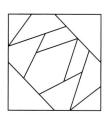

Make 4.

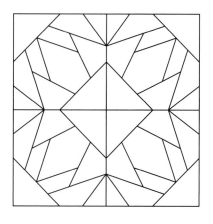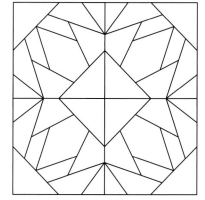

JULIE'S BLOCK

44 PIECES

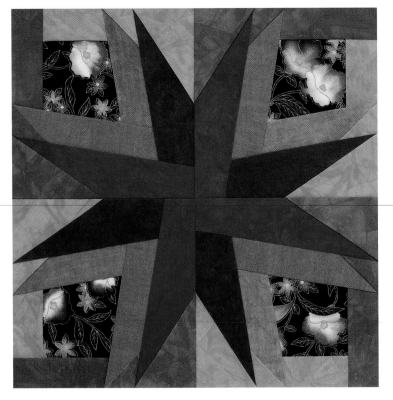
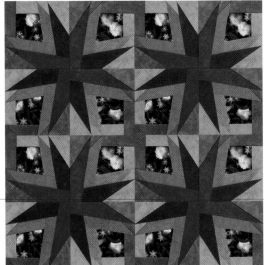

The following cutting list is for one 12" block.

Fabric	No. of Pieces	Dimensions	Location Numbers
Black floral	4	3¼" x 3¼"	1
Light purple	4	1¾" x 5"	4
Light pink	4	1¾" x 6"	5
Medium purple	4	2¼" x 6"	8
Medium pink	4	2¼" x 7"	9
Dark green	4	2½" x 5"	10
	4	1¾" x 4"	3
	4	1½" x 2½"	6
Medium green	4	2½" x 5"	11
	4	1¾" x 3"	2
	4	1½" x 2½"	7

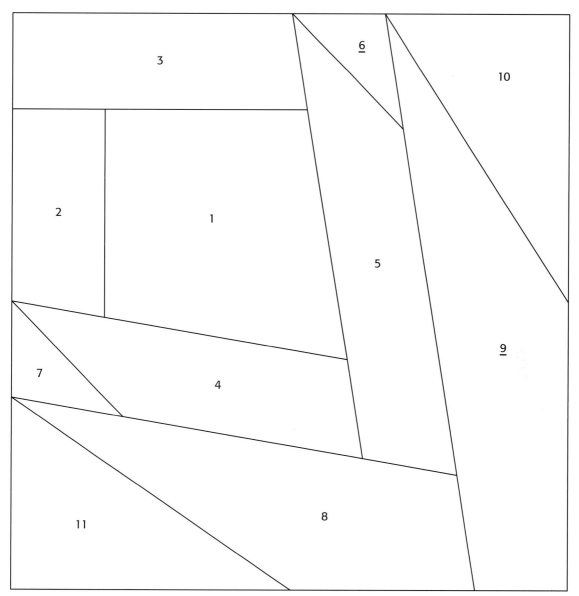

BB20: Julie's Block

Block-Front Drawings

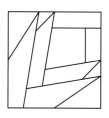

Make 4.

KAREN'S BLOCK

48 PIECES

The following cutting list is for one 12" block.

Fabric	No. of Pieces	Dimensions	Location Numbers
Floral print	4	3¾" x 3¾"	1
	8	2½" x 6¾"	10, 11
	8	2" x 3½"	6, 7
Medium blue	4	2" x 5"	8
Dark blue	4	2½" x 6¾"	9
Light teal	4	1¾" x 2½"	2
Medium teal	8	1¼" x 5"	4, 5
Dark green	2	2¼" x 2¼" ◻	12
	4	1¾" x 3½"	3

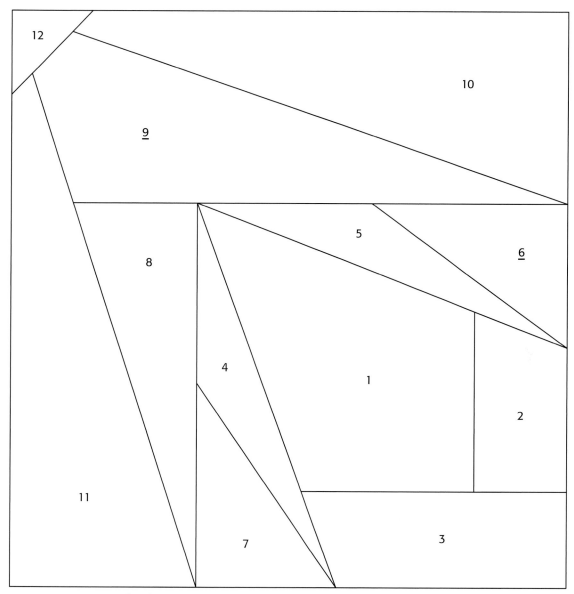

BB21: Karen's Block

Block-Front Drawings

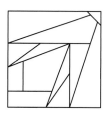

Make 4.

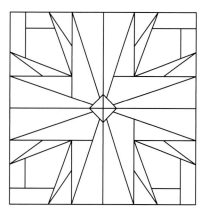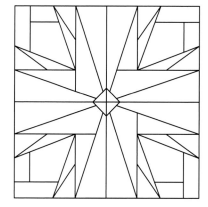

KERRY'S BLOCK

48 PIECES

The following cutting list is for one 12" block.

Fabric	No. of Pieces	Dimensions	Location Numbers
Medium blue	2	2¾" x 2¾" ◻	8
	8	2" x 4"	11, 12
	8	1¾" x 5½"	5, 6
	4	1" x 3"	2
Black	4	1" x 5"	3
White	4	3¼" x 5"	1
Yellow	4	2¾" x 4½"	4
Medium red	4	2" x 6"	7
Dark red	4	2¼" x 6¾"	10
Dark blue	4	2¼" x 5½"	9

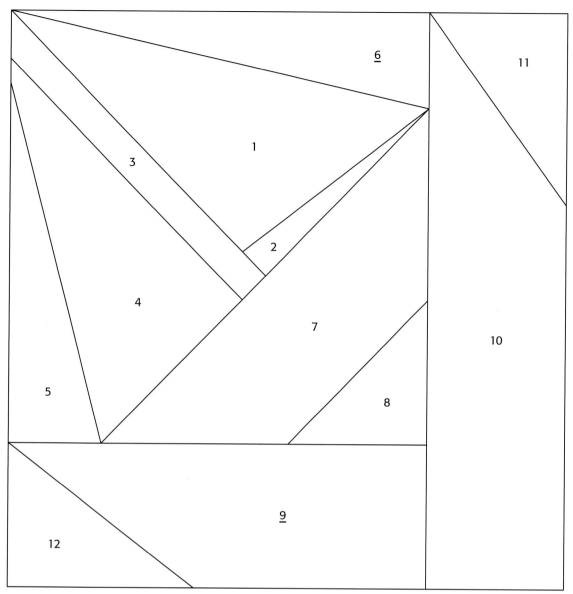

BB22: Kerry's Block

Block-Front Drawings

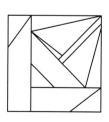

Make 4.

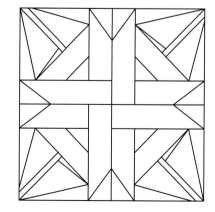

LAUREL'S BLOCK

48 PIECES

The following cutting list is for one 12" block.

Fabric	No. of Pieces	Dimensions	Location Numbers
Floral print	4	5" x 7"	1
Green	8	2" x 5½"	9, 10
	8	1¼" x 5½"	4, 5
Pink	2	2¼" x 2¼" ◻	6
	8	1¾" x 6½"	7, 8
Dark blue	8	1¾" x 4½"	3, 11
Medium blue	8	1¾" x 4½"	2, 12

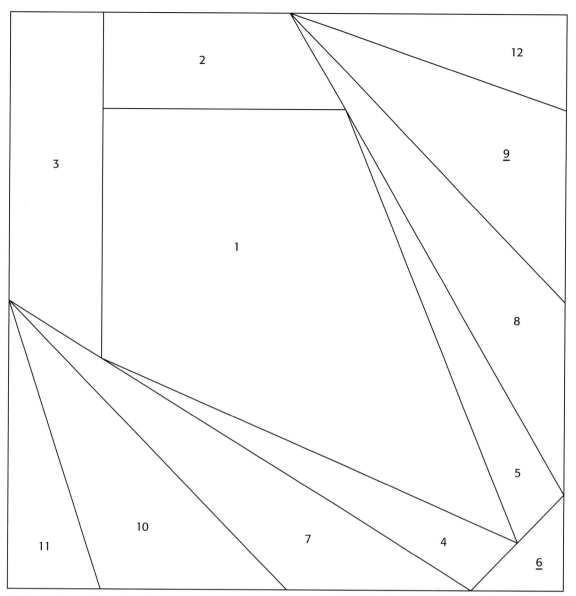

BB23: Laurel's Block

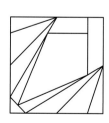

Make 4.

Block-Front Drawings

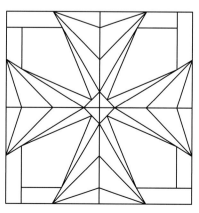

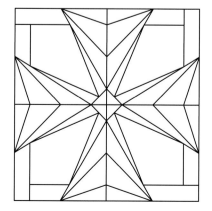

LAURIE'S BLOCK

48 PIECES

The following cutting list is for one 12" block.

Fabric	No. of Pieces	Dimensions	Location Numbers
Print fabric	4	3½" x 6¼"	1
	8	2" x 6½"	7, 8
Dark blue	4	2" x 5½"	3
Medium blue	4	2" x 5"	2
Medium yellow	8	2" x 3½"	4, 5
Light yellow	2	3¼" x 3¼" ◻	6
Dark green	8	2" x 5½"	10, 12
Medium green	8	1½" x 4"	9, 11

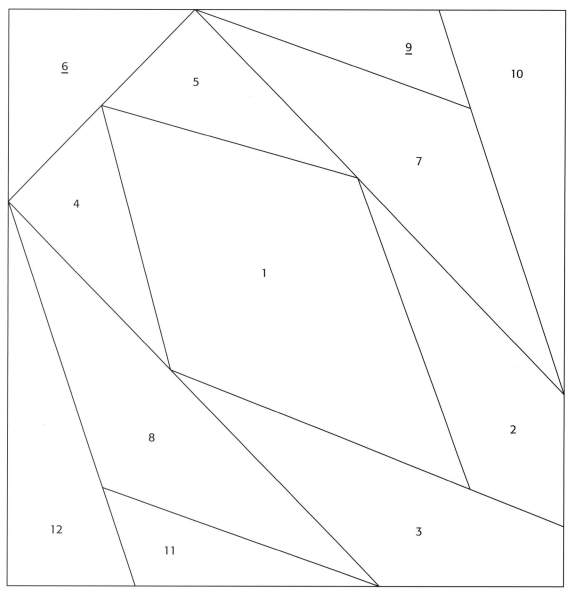

BB24: Laurie's Block

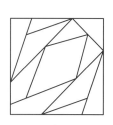

Make 4.

Block-Front Drawings

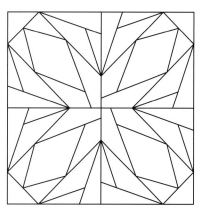

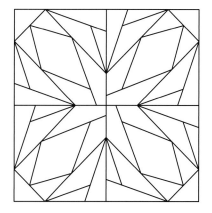

LEANNE'S BLOCK

48 PIECES

The following cutting list is for one 12" block.

Fabric	No. of Pieces	Dimensions	Location Numbers
Rust	4	5" x 5"	8
	4	3¼" x 3¼" ◻	11, 12
	4	2¾" x 2¾" ◻	2, 3
	8	1¼" x 3"	6, 7
Green	8	2" x 7½"	9, 10
Blue #1	4	2¼" x 5½"	5
Blue #2	4	2¼" x 3¾"	4
Gold	4	2¼" x 2¼"	1

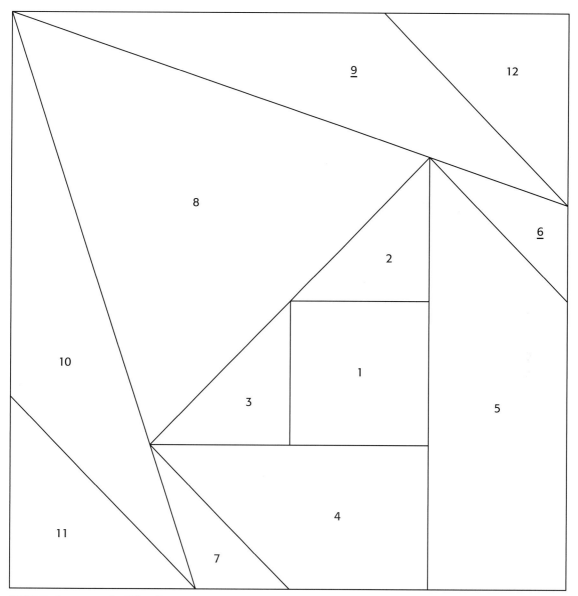

BB25: Leanne's Block

Block-Front Drawings

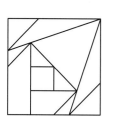

Make 4.

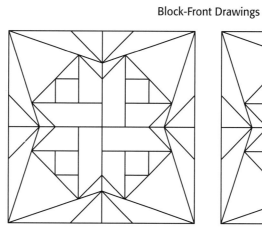

MARY'S BLOCK

48 Pieces

The following cutting list is for one 12" block.

Fabric	No. of Pieces	Dimensions	Location Numbers
Black	4	2¾" x 2¾"	1
	8	2" x 7"	6, 7
	8	1½" x 3½"	10, 11
Print	4	3¼" x 5½"	5
Blue	4	2" x 2¾"	4
Green	2	2¾" x 2¾" ◩	12
	8	2¼" x 6"	8, 9
Dark purple	4	1¾" x 3¾"	3
Medium purple	4	1¾" x 2¾"	2

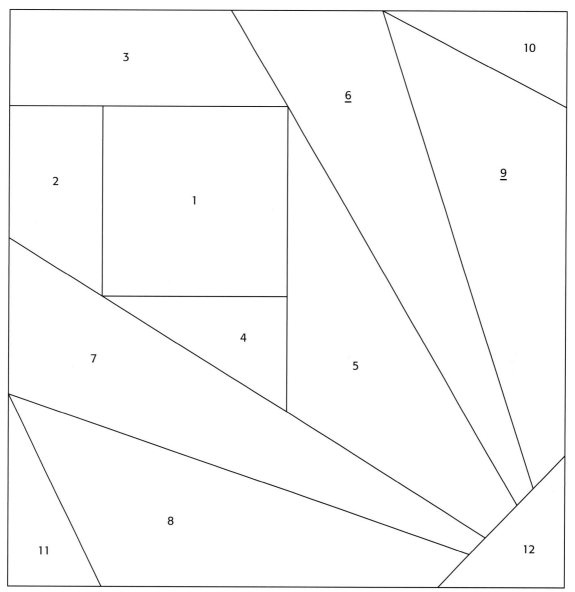

BB26: Mary's Block

Block-Front Drawings

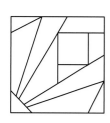

Make 4.

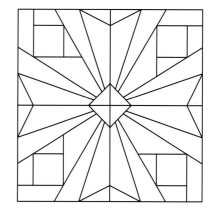

NANCY'S BLOCK

48 PIECES

The following cutting list is for one 12" block.

Fabric	No. of Pieces	Dimensions	Location Numbers
Light blue	2	4¼" x 4¼" ◩	12
	8	2¾" x 2¾" ◩	3, 5, 8, 9
	4	2¼" x 2¼"	1
Yellow check	2	2¾" x 2¾" ◩	2
Yellow dot	4	2¼" x 3¾"	4
Medium pink	4	2¼" x 3¾"	6
Dark pink	4	2¼" x 5¼"	7
Blue check	8	2¼" x 5¼"	10, 11

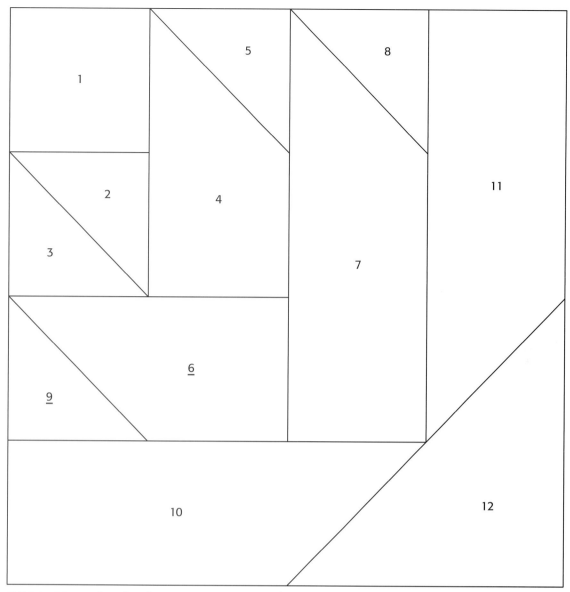

BB28: Nancy's Block

Block-Front Drawings

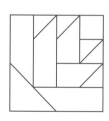

Make 4.

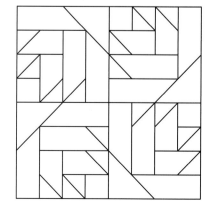

PAM'S BLOCK

52 PIECES

The following cutting list is for one 12" block.

Fabric	No. of Pieces	Dimensions	Location Numbers
Dark blue	12	3¼" x 3¼" ◻	4, 5, 10, 11, 12, 13
	4	2¾" x 2¾"	1
Red #1	4	2¾" x 4¾"	3
Red #2	2	3¼" x 3¼" ◻	2
Lavender	8	1¾" x 4¾"	8, 9
Multicolor batik	8	1¾" x 4¾"	6, 7

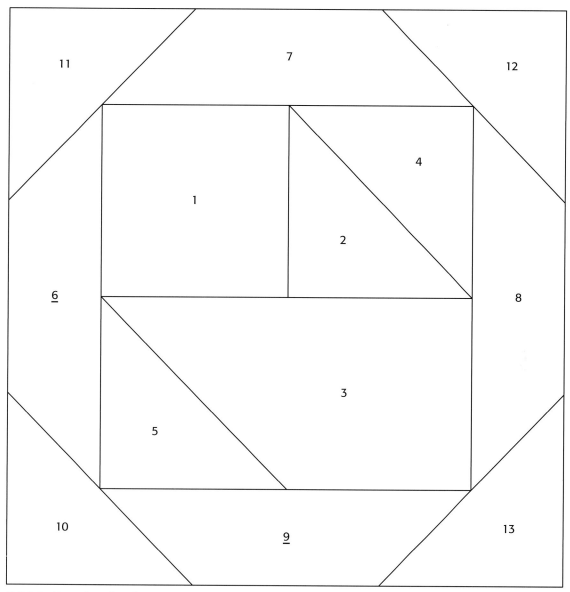

BB29: Pam's Block

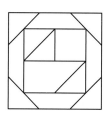

Make 4.

Block-Front Drawings

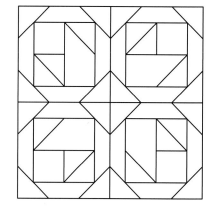

REGINA'S BLOCK

52 PIECES

The following cutting list is for one 12" block.

Fabric	No. of Pieces	Dimensions	Location Numbers
White	4	3¼" x 3¼" ◻	10, 11
	16	2" x 4½"	2, 3, 6, 7
Medium blue	4	3¼" x 3¼" ◻	12, 13
Floral print	4	2" x 6½"	1
Dark purple	8	1¾" x 6½"	4, 5
Fuchsia	8	2" x 5½"	8, 9

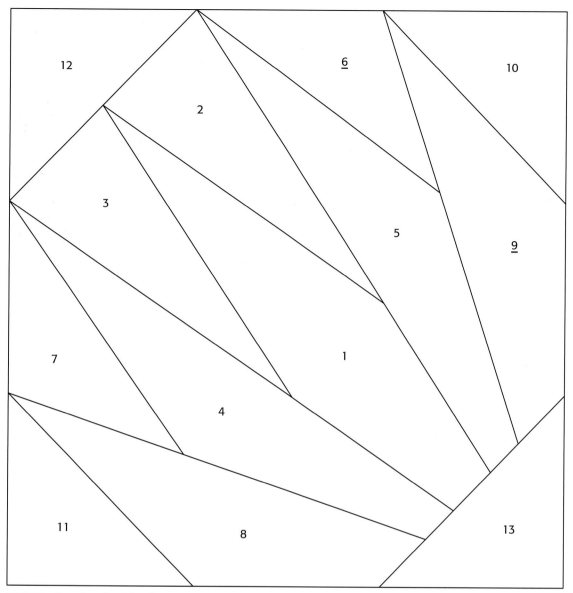

BB30: Regina's Block

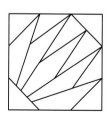

Make 4.

Block-Front Drawings

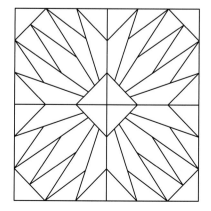

RHODA'S BLOCK

52 PIECES

The following cutting list is for one 12" block.

Fabric	No. of Pieces	Dimensions	Location Numbers
White and green	4	4¼" x 4¼" ◻	10, 11
	4	3¾" x 3¾"	1
Floral print	4	2" x 7"	8
	4	2" x 4¾"	6
Purple	4	2" x 7"	9
	4	2" x 4¾"	7
Dark green	8	2" x 3½"	4, 5
	4	2" x 2" ◻	12, 13
	8	1½" x 2¼"	2, 3

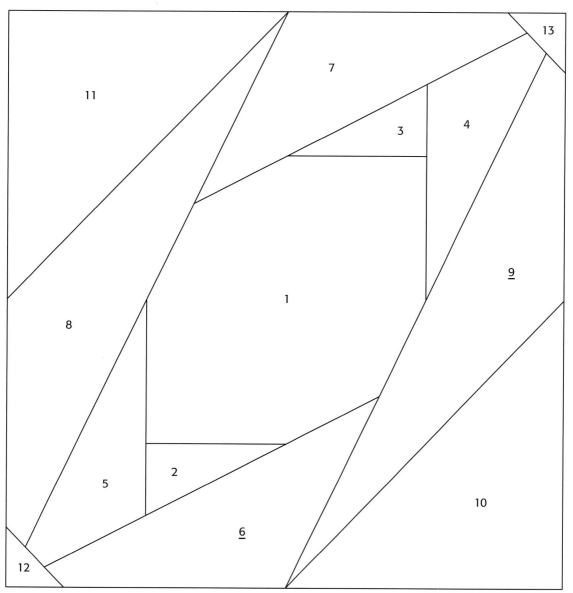

BB31: Rhoda's Block

Block-Front Drawings

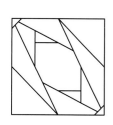

Make 4.

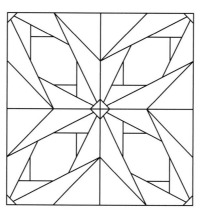
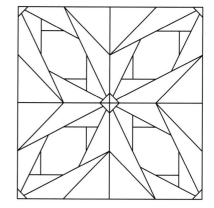

ROBIN'S BLOCK

52 PIECES

The following cutting list is for one 12" block.

Fabric	No. of Pieces	Dimensions	Location Numbers
Black	4	3" x 4"	1
	4	2¾" x 2¾" ⬚	12, 13
	8	1¾" x 3½"	8, 9
Dark blue	4	3" x 5"	5
	4	2½" x 3"	4
Red	8	1½" x 3"	2, 3
Teal	4	1½" x 6"	6
Pink	4	1½" x 6"	7
Yellow	4	2" x 6½"	10
Green	4	2" x 7"	11

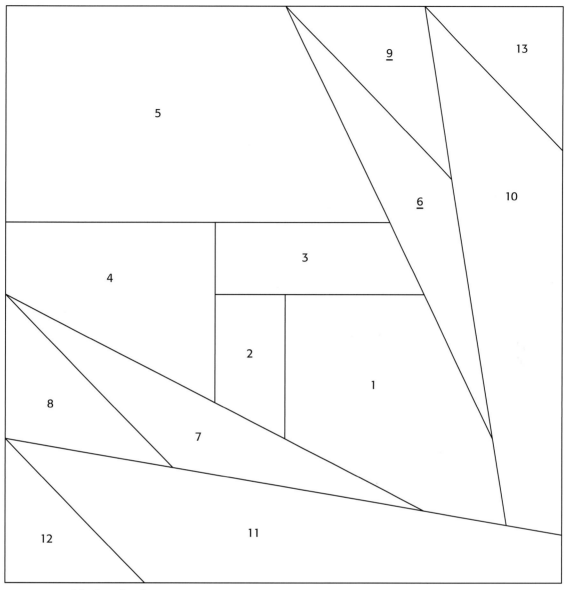

BB32: Robin's Block

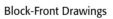

Block-Front Drawings

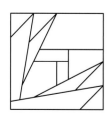

Make 4.

SALLY'S BLOCK

52 PIECES

The following cutting list is for one 12" block.

Fabric	No. of Pieces	Dimensions	Location Numbers
White	4	3¼" x 3¼" ◻	11, 13
Black	16	1½" x 5"	6, 7, 8, 9
Yellow	8	2½" x 5½"	4, 5
	2	3¼" x 3¼" ◻	12
Green	8	2½" x 3¼"	2, 3
Blue	4	2¾" x 5"	1
	2	3¼" x 3¼" ◻	10

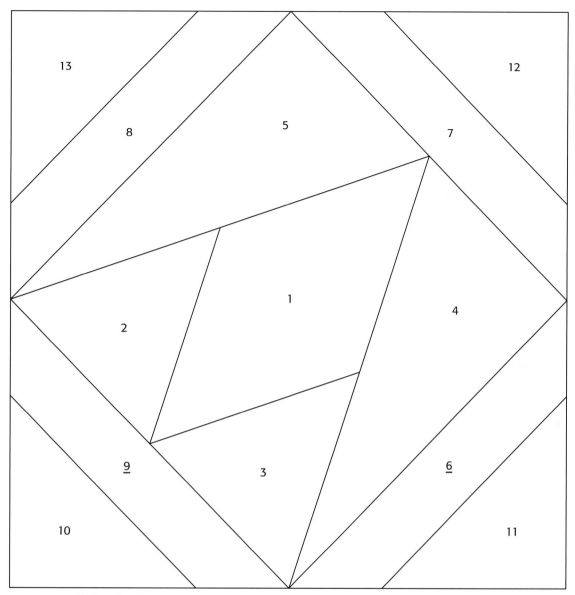

BB33: Sally's Block

Block-Front Drawings

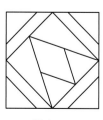

Make 4.

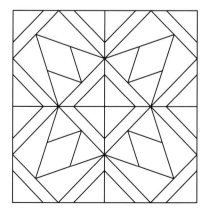

SHARON'S BLOCK

56 PIECES

The following cutting list is for one 12" block.

Fabric	No. of Pieces	Dimensions	Location Numbers
Black	2	3¼" x 3¼" ◻	13
	8	2¼" x 4"	10, 11
	16	1½" x 4"	2, 3, 4, 5
Green #1	4	2¼" x 4½"	1
Green #2	8	2¼" x 3¼"	6, 7
Gold	2	3¼" x 3¼" ◻	14
	4	1½" x 5½"	12
Red	8	2¼" x 5¾"	8, 9

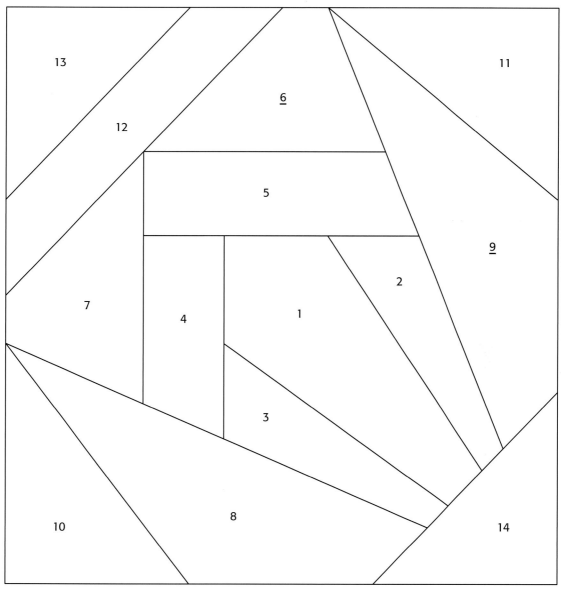

BB34: Sharon's Block

Block-Front Drawings

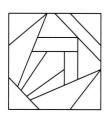

Make 4.

SHEILA'S BLOCK

56 PIECES

The following cutting list is for one 12" block.

Fabric	No. of Pieces	Dimensions	Location Numbers
Blue	4	4¼" x 4¼" ◻	13, 14
	4	3" x 3" ◻	2, 3
	8	1½" x 5½"	11, 12
Green #1	4	1¾" x 4¾"	8
Green #2	4	1¾" x 3¾"	7
Green #3	4	1¾" x 4¾"	6
Green #4	4	1¾" x 3¾"	5
Green #5	2	4¼" x 4¼" ◻	4
Brown	4	1½" x 2¾"	1
Yellow check	4	1¾" x 3¾"	10
Yellow print	4	1¾" x 2¾"	9

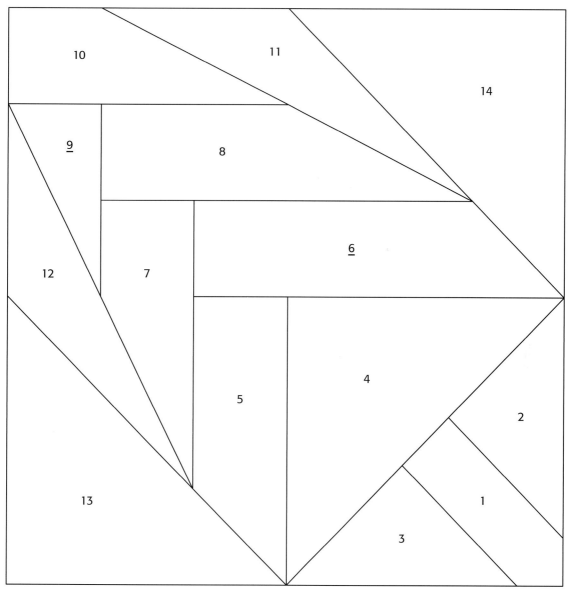

BB35: Sheila's Block

Block-Front Drawings

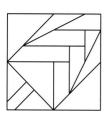

Make 4.

SHERRY'S BLOCK

56 PIECES

The following cutting list is for one 12" block.

Fabric	No. of Pieces	Dimensions	Location Numbers
White print	2	3¼" x 3¼" ◻	14
	4	2¾" x 2¾" ◻	4, 5
	4	1¾" x 5¾"	10
	12	1¾" x 4¾"	9, 11, 12
	4	1¼" x 1¼"	1
Green check	4	2¾" x 6½"	8
Green stripe	12	1¼" x 5½"	6, 7, 13
Dark pink	4	1¾" x 2¼"	3
	4	1¼" x 1¾"	2

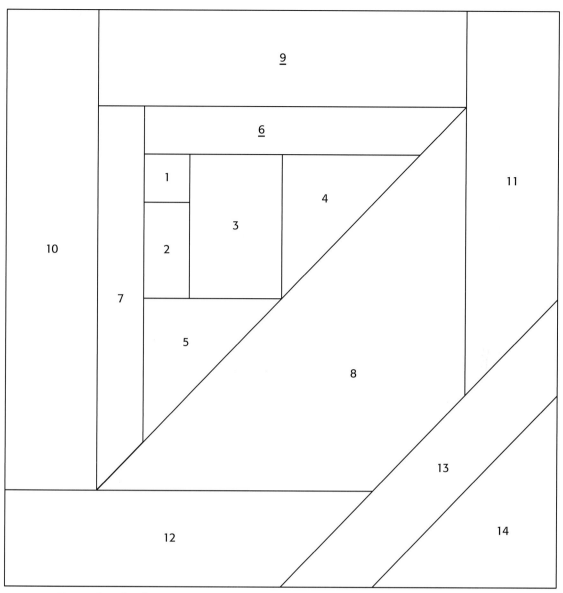

BB36: Sherry's Block

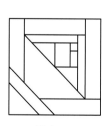

Make 4.

Block-Front Drawings

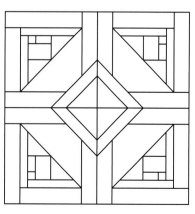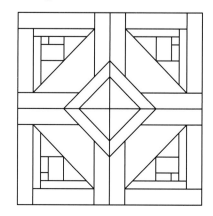

TERRY'S BLOCK

60 PIECES

The following cutting list is for one 12" block.

Fabric	No. of Pieces	Dimensions	Location Numbers
Black	8	2½" x 6¼"	10, 11
	8	2¼" x 2¼" ◻	6, 7, 14, 15
	8	1½" x 3"	2, 3
Blue #1	4	1¾" x 5¾"	12
Blue #2	4	1¾" x 6¾"	13
Green check	4	1¾" x 3¾"	5
Medium green	4	1¾" x 2¾"	4
Yellow	4	2 ¾" x 6"	9
	4	2" x 3¾"	8
Pink	4	2" x 3½"	1

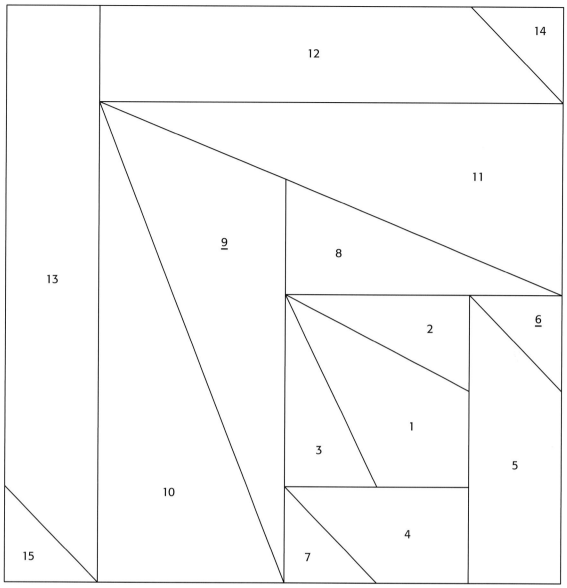

BB37: Terry's Block

Block-Front Drawings

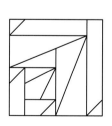

Make 4.

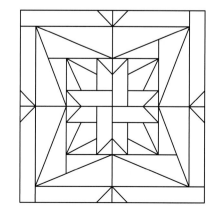

TINA'S BLOCK

64 PIECES

The following cutting list is for one 12" block.

Fabric	No. of Pieces	Dimensions	Location Numbers
Navy	2	4" x 4" ⊠	2, 3
	4	2¼" x 2¼" ⊡	15, 16
	8	1½" x 4½"	8, 9
	8	1½" x 3¼"	5, 6
	8	1¼" x 5¾"	11, 12
Green #1	1	3¾" x 3¾" ⊠	10
Green #2	1	4½" x 4½" ⊠	7
Green #3	1	5½" x 5½" ⊠	4
Gold	4	1¼" x 2¾"	1
Rust #1	4	1¾" x 5¾"	13
Rust #2	4	1¾" x 6¾"	14

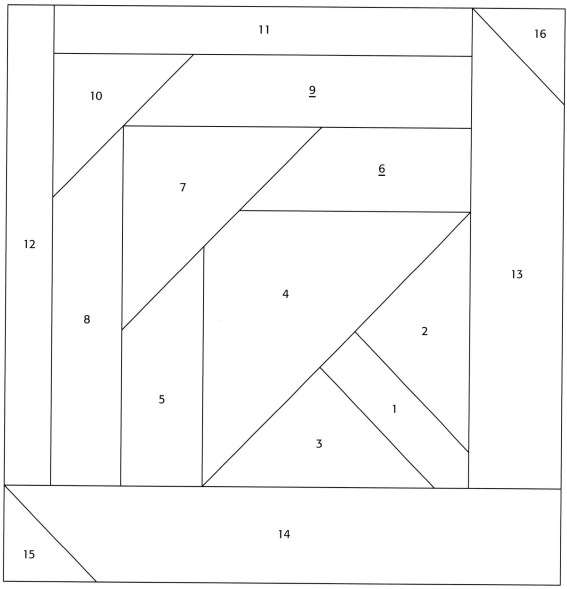

BB38: Tina's Block

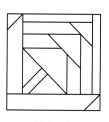

Make 4.

Block-Front Drawings

URSULA'S BLOCK

64 PIECES

The following cutting list is for one 12" block.

Fabric	No. of Pieces	Dimensions	Location Numbers
Light blue	4	4¼" x 4¼" ◻	12, 13
Black	2	3¼" x 3¼" ◻	8
	8	1¾" x 4¾"	14, 15
	4	1½" x 2¼"	5
Medium green	4	1½" x 3½"	9
Blue stripe	4	2¼" x 4¼"	11
Dark green	2	4¼" x 4¼" ◻	16
Red	4	1½" x 3¾"	7
	12	1½" x 2¼"	3, 4, 6
	4	1½" x 1½"	2
Yellow	4	1½" x 1½"	1
Floral fabric	4	2¼" x 2¾"	10

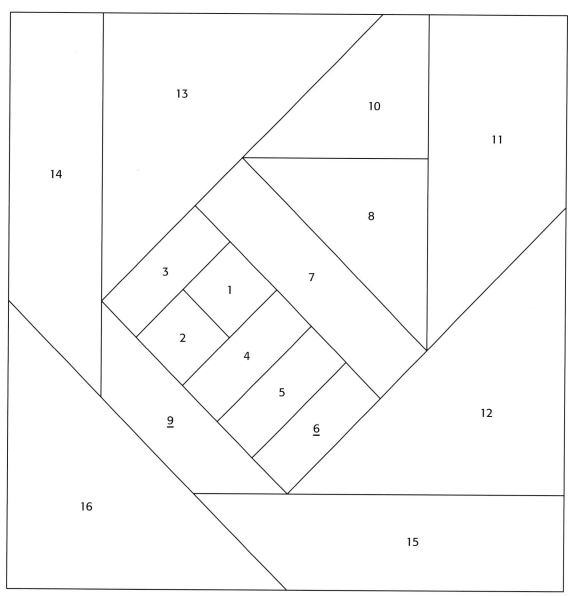

BB39: Ursula's Block

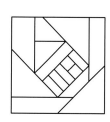

Make 4.

Block-Front Drawings

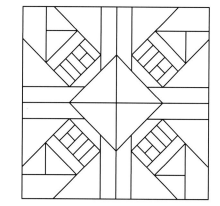

VIRGINIA'S BLOCK

64 PIECES

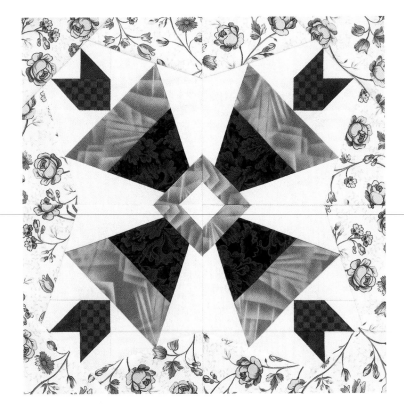

The following cutting list is for one 12" block.

Fabric	No. of Pieces	Dimensions	Location Numbers
Blue and white	2	4¼" x 4¼" ◻	16
	8	2¾" x 5"	14, 15
White	8	2¼" x 3"	6, 7
	8	2" x 4½"	10, 11
	2	2" x 2" ◻	13
	12	1½" x 2¼"	1, 4, 5
Blue #1	2	2¼" x 2¼" ◻	2
Blue #2	4	1¾" x 2¾"	3
Blue #3	4	2" x 5"	8
	4	1¼" x 3½"	12
Blue #4	4	2½" x 3¾"	9

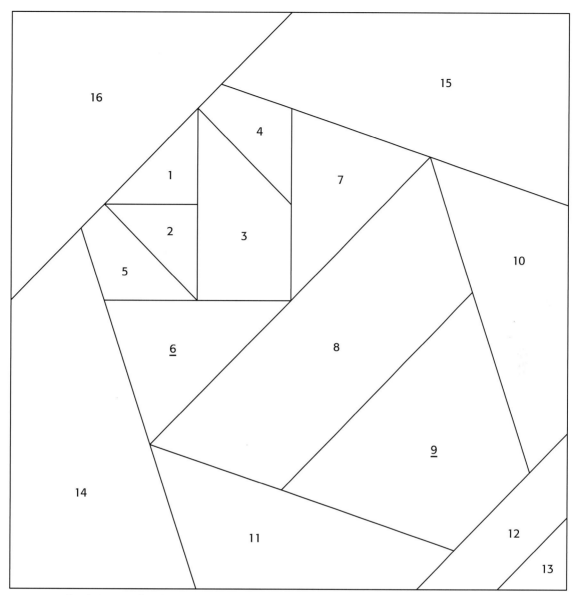

BB40: Virginia's Block

Make 4.

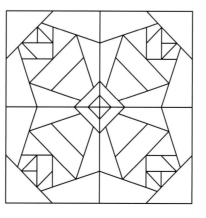

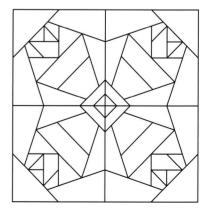

BRIGHT AND BOLD QUILTS

OK, I admit it! I couldn't wait to make quilts using these exciting new block designs. The quilts in this book range from wall-size quilts with just four blocks to bed-size quilts with twenty-five blocks. Each quilt is made with just one block design and includes a single border.

Be sure to read this book all the way through before beginning your quilt, because it contains valuable information and tips to assist you.

- The directions for each quilt include the yardage and a cutting list for each of the fabrics.

- The finished paper-pieced blocks are shown with the corresponding fabric placements and the number of blocks to make.

- The cutting lists indicate the number of pieces to cut, the sizes to cut from each fabric, and where those fabric pieces will be used. When it is a good idea to use nondirectional fabric, I have made that notation in the list of fabrics. In creating the cutting lists, I often rounded up to larger pieces in order to simplify the cutting process.

- When you see the symbol ◻ in the cutting list, cut the squares once diagonally to yield two half-square triangles (see page 11). When you see the symbol ⊠, cut the squares twice diagonally to yield four quarter-square triangles (see pages 11 and 12).

- Border and binding strips are cut either across the width of the fabric or from the length of the fabric as indicated in the cutting chart.

- If you would like to attach a hanging sleeve, add 12" to the yardage requirement for the backing fabric for the first two quilts, and 24" to the yardage requirement for the backing fabric for the remaining quilts.

- Remember to label each group of cut fabrics with the number location, which indicates where the pieces will be used.

ROSE MEDALLION

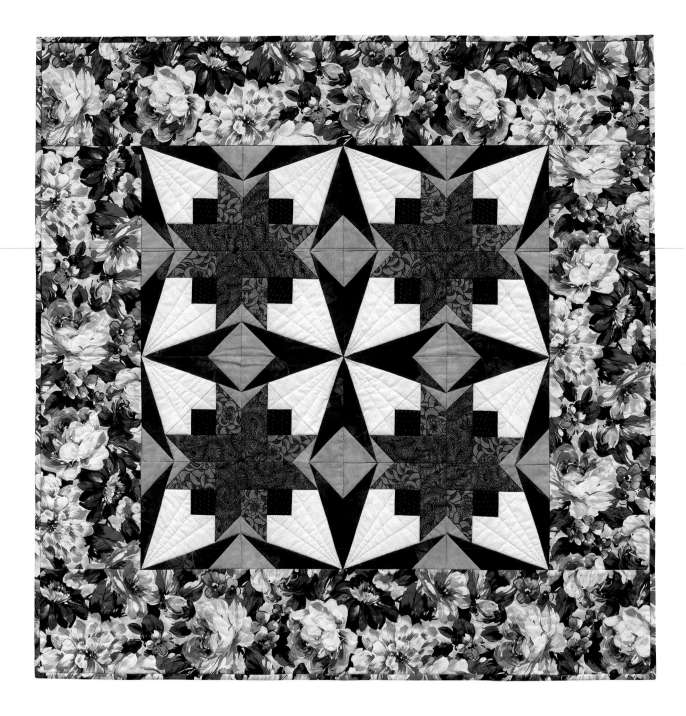

By Carol Doak, 2001, Windham, New Hampshire, 36½" x 36½",
machine quilted by Ellen Peters.

The floral border fabric inspired this combination of colors.
I love the subtle curved impression created by this block.

Fabric and Cutting for Blocks

42"-Wide Fabric	No. of Pieces	Dimensions	Location Numbers
☐ ½ yd. white (nondirectional)	16	5" x 5"	8
	16	2¾" x 2¾" ◻	2, 3
■ ½ yd. dark teal	32	2" x 7½"	9, 10
▦ ⅜ yd. light teal (nondirectional)	16	3¼" x 3¼" ◻	11, 12
	32	1¼" x 3"	6, 7
▦ ¼ yd. dark pink	16	2¼" x 5½"	5
▦ ¼ yd. medium pink	16	2¼" x 3¾"	4
▦ ⅛ yd. black check	16	2¼" x 2¼"	1

Fabric and Cutting for Borders and Binding

Cut across the width of the fabric.

42"-Wide Fabric	No. of Pieces	Dimensions	Location
1⅛ yds. floral print	2	6½" x 24½"	Sides
	2	6½" x 36½"	Top and bottom
	4	2" x 40"	Binding

Additional Materials

1⅛ yds. fabric for backing
40" x 40" piece of batting

1. Make 16 copies of BB25, Leanne's block, on page 70.
2. Make the paper-pieced blocks shown at right.
3. Refer to pages 120–124 to assemble and finish your quilt.

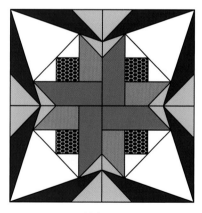

Make 4.

LIGHTED FOREST

By Sherry Reis, 2001, Worthington, Ohio, 36½" x 36½".

This combination of warm and cool batik fabrics is subtle, yet dramatic. The simple radiating pattern is enhanced with Sherry's decorative hand quilting.

Fabric and Cutting for Blocks

42"-Wide Fabric	No. of Pieces	Dimensions	Location Numbers
▢ ½ yd. light green	16	4¼" x 4¼" ◨	6, 7*
	16	3¾" x 3¾"	1
▨ ½ yd. teal	16	2¼" x 5½"	3
	16	1¾" x 3¾"	2
▢ ⅜ yd. light gold	16	2½" x 6½"	4
▨ ⅜ yd. medium gold	16	2½" x 7½"	5

*In order for the directional fabric to be consistent for these triangles, creating the woven look, cut the squares and cut on the diagonal line in the same direction, with the right side of the fabric facing up. Place the light green fabric as shown in the illustration at right for all blocks.

Cut half-square triangles.

Place squares and triangles as shown.

Fabric and Cutting for Borders and Binding

Cut across the width of the fabric.

Fabric	No. of Pieces	Dimensions	Location
1⅛ yds. dark green batik	2	6½" x 24½"	Sides
	2	6½" x 36½"	Top/bottom
	4	2" x 40"	Binding

Additional Materials

  1⅛ yds. fabric for backing
  40" x 40" piece of batting

1. Make 16 copies of BB2, Barbara's block, on page 24.
2. Make the paper-pieced blocks shown at right.
3. Refer to pages 120–124 to assemble and finish your quilt.

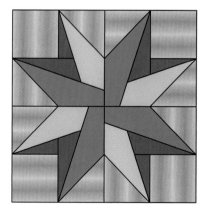

Make 4.

WOVEN STARS

By Carol Doak, 2001, Windham, New Hampshire, 48½" x 48½",
machine quilted by Ellen Peters.

*The Asian-looking border fabric inspired the color combination used in the
blocks. The special placement of purple fabrics creates interesting woven stars.*

Fabric and Cutting for Blocks

	42"-Wide Fabric	No. of Pieces	Dimensions	Location Numbers
☐	⅝ yd. white	36	4¼" x 4¼" ◺	8 (A, B, C, D); 9 (A, B, C, D)
■	⅜ yd. black	36	2¾" x 2¾"	1 (A, B, C, D)
		18	2¼" x 2¼" ◺	10 (A, B, C, D)
▨	¼ yd. light pink	36	1¾" x 3"	2 (A, B, C, D)
▨	½ yd. medium pink	36	2½" x 5"	4 (A, B, C, D)
■	⅞ yd. green	72	2" x 7"	6 (A, B, C, D); 7 (A, B, C, D)
▨	¼ yd. purple #1	9	2¾" x 5"	5A
		9	2¾" x 2¾"	3B
▨	¼ yd. purple #2	9	2¾" x 5"	5B
		9	2¾" x 2¾"	3C
▨	¼ yd. purple #3	9	2¾" x 5"	5C
		9	2¾" x 2¾"	3D
■	¼ yd. purple #4	9	2¾" x 5"	5D
		9	2¾" x 2¾"	3A

Fabric and Cutting for Borders and Binding

Cut from the length of the fabric.

Fabric	No. of Pieces	Dimensions	Location
1½ yds. print	2	6½" x 36½"	Sides
	2	6½" x 48½"	Top and bottom
	4	2" x 51"	Binding

Additional Materials

3 yds. fabric for backing
52" x 52" piece of batting

Note: The fabric placement for location numbers 3 and 5 will change for each of the four blocks. To place fabrics in the proper positions, label 9 foundations with A, 9 with B, 9 with C, and 9 with D.

1. Make 36 copies of BB12, Dawn's block, on page 44.
2. Make the paper-pieced blocks shown at right.

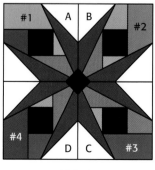

Make 9.

3. Refer to pages 120–124 to assemble and finish your quilt.

TOWN SQUARE

By Carol Doak, 2001, Windham, New Hampshire, 48½" x 48½",
machine quilted by Ellen Peters.

*I had such fun making these house blocks. I love the way they meet with a
town square in the middle and are connected with what appear to be roads.*

Fabric and Cutting for Blocks

42"-Wide Fabric	No. of Pieces	Dimensions	Location Numbers
⁵⁄₈ yd. white	36	4¼" x 4¼" ◺	12, 13
¾ yd. navy	18	3¼" x 3¼" ◺	8
	72	1¾" x 4¾"	14, 15
	36	1½" x 2¼"	5
¼ yd. light green	36	1½" x 3½"	9
⅓ yd. green print	36	2¼" x 4¼"	11
⅓ yd. medium green	18	4¼" x 4¼" ◺	16
⅝ yd. yellow	36	1½" x 3¾"	7
	108	1½" x 2¼"	3, 4, 6
	36	1½" x 1½"	2
⅛ yd. small blue check	36	1½" x 1½"	1
¼ yd. medium blue	36	2¼ x 2¾"	10

Fabric and Cutting for Borders and Binding

Cut from the length of the fabric.

Fabric	No. of Pieces	Dimensions	Location
1½ yds. print	2	6½" x 36½"	Sides
	2	6½" x 48½"	Top and bottom
	4	2" x 51"	Binding

Additional Materials

3 yds. fabric for backing
52" x 52" piece of batting

1. Make 36 copies of BB39, Ursula's block, on page 98.
2. Make the paper-pieced blocks shown at right.
3. Refer to pages 120–124 to assemble and finish your quilt.

Make 9.

111

BURST OF SPRING

By Carol Doak, 2001, Windham, New Hampshire, 60½" x 60½",
machine quilted by Ellen Peters.

*The festive floral border was the perfect inspiration for using
a variety of solid-color flowers to add interest to this quilt.*

Fabric and Cutting for Blocks

42"-Wide Fabric	No. of Pieces	Dimensions	Location Numbers
☐ 3 yds. white	64	2¾" x 2¾"	1
	128	2½" x 5"	9, 10
	128	1½" x 4"	4, 5
	14	1¾" x 42"	pieced unit 6*
	2	1¾" x 6"	pieced unit 6*
■ 1⅔ yds. dark green	128	2½" x 7"	7, 8
■ ½ yd. green check	32	2¼" x 2¼" ◻	11
	7	1¼" x 42"	pieced unit 6*
	1	1¼" x 6"	pieced unit 6*
▨ ¼ yd. each of 8 asst. solids	*From each color:*		
	2	5½" x 5½" ⊠	3
	4	3¼" x 3¼" ◻	2

*Piece strips as shown and crosscut into segments, each 4¼" wide, to make 64 pieced units. After joining pieced unit 6, press open and machine baste in position to the foundation across the bottom (see page 18).

← 4¼" →

Make 7 strips sets each 42" long
and 1 strip set 6" long.
Cut a total of 64 segments.

Fabric and Cutting for Borders and Binding

Cut from the length of the fabric.

Fabric	No. of Pieces	Dimensions	Location
1⅞ yds. print	2	6½" x 48½"	Sides
	2	6½" x 60½"	Top and bottom
	4	2" x 63"	Binding

Additional Materials

3⅝ yds. fabric for backing
64" x 64" piece of batting

1. Make 64 copies of BB16, Ginny's block, on page 52.
2. Make the paper-pieced blocks shown at right.
3. Refer to pages 120–124 to assemble and finish your quilt.

Make 16.

113

FLOWER WEAVE

By Carol Doak, 2001, Windham, New Hampshire, 60½" x 60½",
machine quilted by Ellen Peters.

*This graphic quilt has an elegant look, with several secondary
patterns to hold your interest throughout.*

Fabric and Cutting for Blocks

42"-Wide Fabric	No. of Pieces	Dimensions	Location Numbers
2½ yds. white	128	2½" x 6¼"	10, 11
	128	2¼" x 2¼" ◻	6, 7, 14, 15
	128	1½" x 3"	2, 3
1 yd. dark green	64	1¾" x 6¾"	13
	64	1¾" x 3¾"	5
⅞ yd. medium green	64	1¾" x 5¾"	12
	64	1¾" x 2¾"	4
½ yd. light pink	64	2" x 3¾"	8
1 yd. medium pink	64	2¾" x 6"	9
½ yd. dark pink	64	2" x 3½"	1

Fabric and Cutting for Borders and Binding

Cut from the length of the fabric.

Fabric	No. of Pieces	Dimensions	Location
1⅞ yds. pink floral	2	6½" x 48½"	Sides
	2	6½" x 60½"	Top and bottom
	4	2" x 63"	Binding

Additional Materials

3⅝ yds. fabric for backing
64" x 64" piece of batting

1. Make 64 copies of BB37, Terry's block, on page 94.
2. Make the paper-pieced blocks shown at right.
3. Refer to pages 120–124 to assemble and finish your quilt.

Make 16.

SEASIDE

By Carol Doak, Windham, New Hampshire, and Sherry Reis,
Worthington, Ohio, 2001, 72½" x 72½", machine quilted by Ellen Peters.

*The multicolor batik border fabric inspired the combination of colors
used in the blocks. The open areas in the center of the blocks provide
the perfect place to feature some decorative quilting.*

Fabric and Cutting for Blocks

	42"-Wide Fabric	No. of Pieces	Dimensions	Location Numbers
☐	1¾ yds. yellow	100	4¾" x 4¾"	1
■	1⅛ yds. dark blue	200	1½" x 4"	6, 7
■	2¼ yds. medium blue	200	2½" x 5¾"	8, 9
■	¾ yd. dark orange	100	1¾" x 4¾"	5
■	⅝ yd. light orange	100	1¾" x 3¾"	2
■	¾ yd. medium teal	100	1¾" x 4¾"	4
☐	⅝ yd. light teal	100	1¾" x 3¾"	3

Fabric and Cutting for Borders and Binding

Cut from the length of the fabric.

Fabric	No. of Pieces	Dimensions	Location
2¼ yds. print	2	6½" x 60½"	Sides
	2	6½" x 72½"	Top and bottom
	4	2" x 75"	Binding

Additional Materials

4⅜ yds. fabric for backing
76" x 76" piece of batting

1. Make 100 copies of BB10, Cleo's block, on page 40.
2. Make the paper-pieced blocks shown at right.
3. Refer to pages 120–124 to assemble and finish your quilt.

Make 25.

SPINNERS

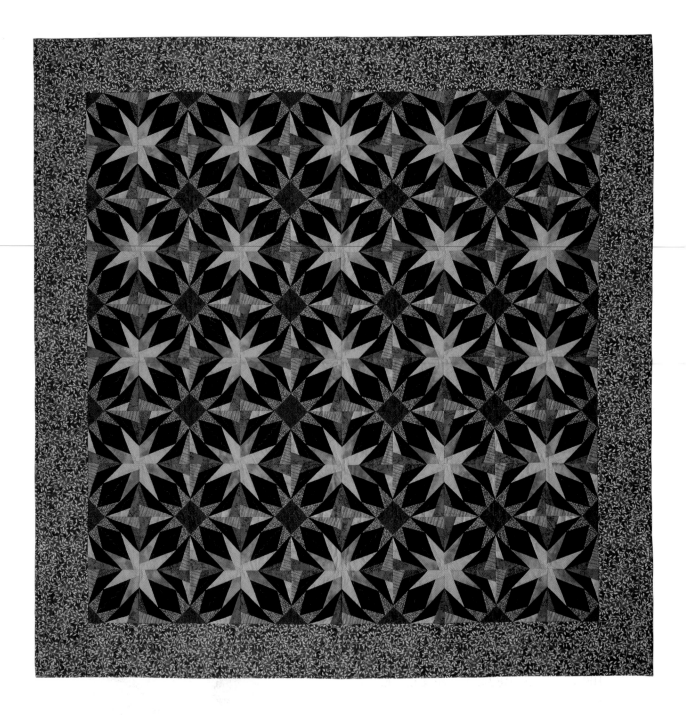

By Carol Doak, 2001, Windham, New Hampshire, 72½" x 72½",
machine quilted by Ellen Peters.

*This quilt surprised even me. When sewing the blocks together, I found that I couldn't take
my eyes off the partially completed quilt on the wall because the variety of bright colors
and different-shaped stars held my interest on so many levels. I love the result!*

Fabric and Cutting for Blocks

	42"-Wide Fabric	No. of Pieces	Dimensions	Location Numbers
■	3¾ yds. black (nondirectional)	100	3½" x 6¼"	1
		200	2" x 6½"	7, 8
■	1 yd. yellow	100	2" x 5½"	3
■	⅞ yd. orange	100	2" x 5"	2
■	1⅛ yds. medium green	200	2" x 3½"	4, 5
■	⅝ yd. dark green	50	3¼" x 3¼" ◻	6
■	1 yd. medium blue	100	2" x 5½"	10
■	½ yd. light blue	100	1½" x 4"	9
■	1 yd. light purple	100	2" x 5½"	12
■	½ yd. medium purple	100	1½" x 4"	11

Fabric and Cutting for Borders and Binding

Cut from the length of the fabric.

Fabric	No. of Pieces	Dimensions	Location
2¼ yds. print	2	6½" x 60½"	Sides
	2	6½" x 72½"	Top and bottom
	4	2" x 75"	Binding

Additional Materials

4⅜ yds. fabric for backing
76" x 76" piece of batting

1. Make 100 copies of BB24, Laurie's block, on page 68.
2. Make the paper-pieced blocks shown at right.
3. Refer to pages 120–124 to assemble and finish your quilt.

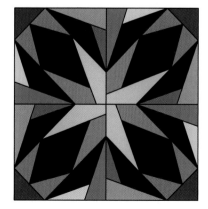

Make 25.

119

QUILT ASSEMBLY AND FINISHING

Arrange the blocks as shown in the photograph for the quilt and sew the blocks together in horizontal rows. Press the middle horizontal seam in each 12" x 12" block in opposite directions from row to row. Press the vertical seam allowances for the joined blocks in opposite directions from row to row. Join the rows. Press the horizontal seams of the joined rows in one direction. Don't forget to machine baste the beginning, the middle, and any matching points before joining blocks and rows.

ADDING BORDERS

The quilts in this book are made with straight-cut corners. The border measurements for each quilt are supplied, but you will want to double-check these measurements against your completed patchwork. Measure the length of the quilt top at the center, from raw edge to raw edge, and cut two border strips to match that measurement. Mark the centers of the border strips and the sides of the quilt top. Join the borders to the sides, matching center marks and edges and easing as necessary. Press the seam allowances toward the borders.

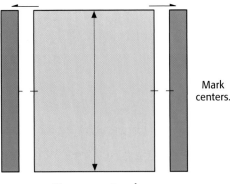

Mark centers.

Measure center of quilt, top to bottom.

Measure the width of the quilt top through the center from raw edge to raw edge, including the border pieces just added. Cut two border strips to match that measurement. Mark the centers of the border strips and top and bottom of the quilt top. Join the border strips to the top and bottom edges, matching centers and ends and easing as necessary. Press the seams toward the borders.

Measure center of quilt, side to side, including borders.

Mark centers.

REMOVING THE PAPER

It is now time to remove the paper. Reserve this activity for evening relaxing time as it is a mindless task. Starting at the outside perimeter of the quilt, gently tug against the seam lines to pull the paper away from the stitching. Use a pair of tweezers to remove the paper from the intersecting seams.

CUTTING THE BACKING AND BATTING

The first two quilts are 36" wide, so they will require one length of fabric for the backing. The remaining quilts require that you join two lengths of fabric to create the backing. Cut two lengths of fabric the length of the quilt, plus about 4". Remove the selvages from both lengths. Sew the pieces together with a ¼"-wide seam allowance, or split one piece lengthwise and sew the resulting pieces to either side of the other length. Press the seam allowances open.

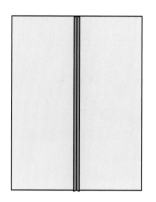 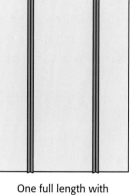

Two lengths with center seam

One full length with two partial lengths on each side

Cut the batting to the size of the quilt top, plus another 2" to 4".

BASTING AND QUILTING

To baste the backing, batting, and quilt top together:

1. Spread the backing, wrong side up, on a clean surface. You can use the floor or a table, depending on the size of the project. Being careful not to stretch the backing out of shape, anchor it to your work surface. If you're working on a carpet, use pins; if you are working on a hard surface, use masking tape.

2. Spread and smooth the batting over the backing, making sure batting covers the backing evenly.

3. Center the quilt top on the batting, right side up, smoothing out any wrinkles. Make sure the edges of the quilt top are parallel to the edges of the backing.

4. If you plan to hand quilt, begin basting from the center to the outside edge. Make vertical and horizontal rows of basting stitches about

5" to 8" apart and two diagonal rows from corner to corner. If you plan to machine quilt, pin-baste from the center to the outside edge, using size 1 or 2 rustproof safety pins and placing them about 4" apart.

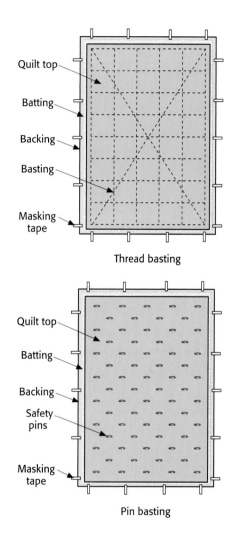

Thread basting

Pin basting

5. Bring the edge of the backing over the edge of the exposed batting and baste to the top of quilt.

The quilts in this book can be hand quilted or machine quilted. Save intricate quilting designs for open areas, where they can be appreciated. Begin quilting in the middle of the quilt and work toward the outside edges in a consistent fashion.

ADDING A SLEEVE

If you want to hang your quilt, baste a sleeve to the quilt before adding the binding.

1. Cut a strip of fabric as long as the width of the quilt (or join 2 strips if needed) and double the desired depth of the sleeve, adding ½" for seam allowances. Hem both ends of the strip.

2. Fold the strip, wrong sides together, and pin the raw edges at the top of the quilt before you attach the binding. Machine baste in place ⅛" from the edge. Add the binding to the quilt.

3. Blindstitch the folded edge of the sleeve to the back of the quilt.

BINDING THE EDGES

Once you have completed the quilting, prepare the quilt for binding by removing the basting stitches (or safety pins) and trimming the batting and backing even with the edges of the quilt top. Adjust your machine for a basting-length stitch and use a walking foot or even-feed foot, if available, to stitch around the perimeter of the quilt sandwich approximately ⅛" from the edge. The even-feed foot aids in sewing all three layers smoothly. If you are adding a sleeve to hang the quilt, baste it in place now (see "Adding a Sleeve" above).

The directions for the quilts include information for cutting straight-grain binding strips. Join the ends of the strips at a 45° angle to make a strip long enough to go around the perimeter of the quilt, plus about 10". Trim the excess fabric, press the seams open, and clip the "dog-ears."

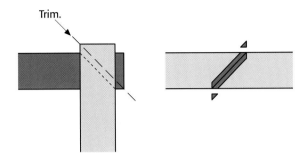

To attach the binding:

1. Place the binding strip, wrong side up, on the cutting mat. Align a rotary ruler's 45°-angle marking with the edge of the strip near one end. Draw a cutting line.

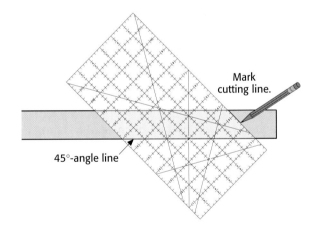

Mark cutting line.

45°-angle line

Turn the strip and draw two more lines, each ¼" from the previous line.

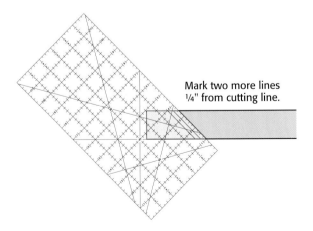

Mark two more lines ¼" from cutting line.

The first line is the cutting line, the second is the sewing line, and the third is the measuring line. Cut on the cutting line.

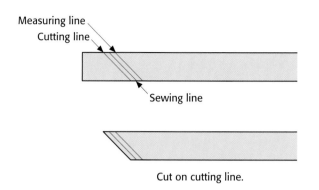

Measuring line
Cutting line
Sewing line

Cut on cutting line.

2. Fold the strip in half lengthwise, wrong sides together, and press.

3. Place the binding on the front of the quilt, in the middle of the bottom edge, aligning the raw edges of the binding with the edge of the quilt. Attach a walking foot or even-feed foot to your sewing machine. Starting about 6" from the end of the binding, sew the binding to the quilt with a ¼"-wide seam allowance. Stop stitching ¼" from the corner of the quilt and backstitch.

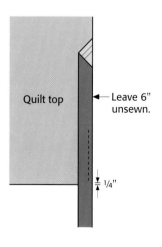

Quilt top

Leave 6" unsewn.

¼"

4. Turn the quilt to sew the next edge. Fold the binding up, away from the quilt, and then down, even with the next side. The straight fold should be even with the upper edge of the quilt.

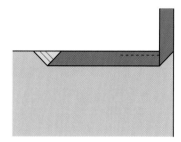

5. Stitch from the edge to the next corner, stopping ¼" from the corner. Repeat for the remaining corners.

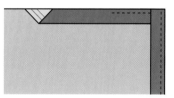

6. After the last corner is stitched, stop. Unfold the strip and place it under the beginning of the binding. On the wrong side, mark the raw edge of the strip at the measuring line on the beginning strip.

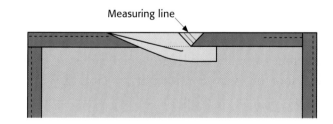

Measuring line

7. Align the rotary ruler's 45° line with the straight edge of the end tail, placing the edge of the ruler at the mark. Draw a cutting line. Draw a sewing line ¼" away as shown. Place the binding strip on the cutting table, away from the quilt, and cut on the cutting line.

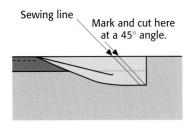

Sewing line
Mark and cut here at a 45° angle.

Wrong side of binding strip

8. Pull the ends of the binding strips away from the quilt. Place the unfolded strips right sides together as shown. Pin, matching the two sewing lines, and stitch. Press the seam allowances open. Clip the dog-ears and lightly press the strip in half again.

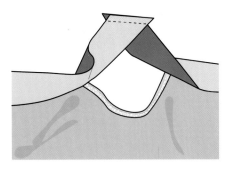

9. Return the strip to the edge of the quilt and finish the seam.

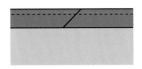

10. Fold the binding to the back, over the raw edges of the quilt. The folded edge of the binding should cover the machine stitching lines. Blindstitch the binding in place.

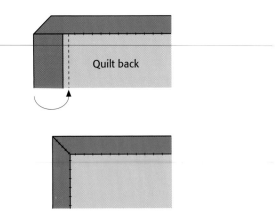

Quilt back

RESOURCES

Papers for Foundation Piecing
Martingale & Company
20205 144th Avenue NE
Woodinville, WA 98072-8478
Telephone: 800-426-3126
Web site: www.martingale-pub.com

Add-a-Quarter Ruler
C M Designs
7968 Kelty Trail
Franktown, CO 80116
Telephone: 303-841-5920

Information about the thread-clipping snips is available from:

Tool-Tron Industries
Telephone: 830-249-8277
Web site: www.Tooltron.com
E-mail: tooltron@texas.net

The companion computer program for *40 Bright and Bold Paper-Pieced Blocks* allows you to print the block designs from this book. It is *only* available through Quilt-Pro Systems at the following address, phone, or Internet site:

Quilt-Pro Systems, Inc.
PO Box 560692
The Colony, TX 75056
Telephone: 800-884-1511

Or order via a credit card on the Web at: www.CarolDoak.com/order

System Requirements: Windows 95/98/NT4, 2000, ME, or XP; 8 MB RAM; 25 MB available disk space; and mouse or other pointing device. High-color or true-color video recommended.

Carol Doak's teaching schedule is available on her Web site at the following address:
http://quilt.com/CDoak

ABOUT THE AUTHOR

As a bestselling author and celebrated teacher, Carol Doak has greatly influenced the art and craft of quiltmaking for more than a decade, both in the United States and internationally. Her accomplishments include a sizable collection of popular books: *Easy Machine Paper Piecing, Easy Paper-Pieced Keepsake Quilts, Easy Mix & Match Machine Paper Piecing, Show Me How to Paper Piece, Easy Reversible Vests, Easy Paper-Pieced Miniatures, Your First Quilt Book (or it should be!), Easy Stash Quilts, 50 Fabulous Paper-Pieced Stars* and *Easy Paper-Pieced Baby Quilts.* It is no secret that Carol has helped to raise the popularity of paper piecing, her trademark technique, worldwide.

An impressive range of Carol's blue-ribbon quilts have been featured in several books, such as *Great American Quilts 1990* and *The Quilt Encyclopedia*, and on the covers of *Quilter's Newsletter Magazine, Quilt World, Quilting Today, Lady's Circle Patchwork Quilts,* and *McCall's Quilting.*

If you have ever taken a class from Carol, you know that her enthusiasm for quiltmaking is infectious. She has a gift for sharing her inspiring ideas and techniques with her students in a positive and unique way.

Carol lives with her husband in Windham, New Hampshire, where the cold winters offer plenty of opportunity to snuggle under a quilt in progress.

new and bestselling titles from

America's Best-Loved Craft & Hobby Books™

America's Best-Loved Quilt Books®

NEW RELEASES
All Through the Woods
American Quilt Classics
Amish Wall Quilts
Animal Kingdom CD-ROM
Batik Beauties
The Casual Quilter
Fantasy Floral Quilts
Fast Fusible Quilts
Friendship Blocks
From the Heart
Log Cabin Fever
Machine-Stitched Cathedral Stars
Magical Hexagons
Potting Shed Patchwork
Repliqué Quilts

APPLIQUÉ
Artful Album Quilts
Artful Appliqué
Colonial Appliqué
Red and Green: An Appliqué Tradition
Rose Sampler Supreme

BABY QUILTS
Easy Paper-Pieced Baby Quilts
Even More Quilts for Baby: Easy as ABC
More Quilts for Baby: Easy as ABC
Play Quilts
The Quilted Nursery
Quilts for Baby: Easy as ABC

HOLIDAY QUILTS
Christmas at That Patchwork Place
Holiday Collage Quilts
Paper Piece a Merry Christmas
A Snowman's Family Album Quilt
Welcome to the North Pole

LEARNING TO QUILT
Basic Quiltmaking Techniques for:
   Borders and Bindings
   Divided Circles
   Hand Appliqué
   Machine Appliqué
   Strip Piecing
The Joy of Quilting
The Simple Joys of Quilting
Your First Quilt Book (or it should be!)

PAPER PIECING
50 Fabulous Paper-Pieced Stars
For the Birds
Paper Piece a Flower Garden
Paper-Pieced Bed Quilts
Paper-Pieced Curves
A Quilter's Ark
Show Me How to Paper Piece

ROTARY CUTTING
101 Fabulous Rotary-Cut Quilts
365 Quilt Blocks a Year Perpetual Calendar
Around the Block Again
Biblical Blocks
Creating Quilts with Simple Shapes
Flannel Quilts
More Fat Quarter Quilts
More Quick Watercolor Quilts
Razzle Dazzle Quilts

SCRAP QUILTS
Nickel Quilts
Scrap Frenzy
Scrappy Duos
Spectacular Scraps

CRAFTS
The Art of Stenciling
Baby Dolls and Their Clothes
Creating with Paint
Creepy Crafty Halloween
The Decorated Kitchen
The Decorated Porch
A Handcrafted Christmas
Painted Chairs
Sassy Cats

KNITTING & CROCHET
Clever Knits
Crochet for Babies and Toddlers
Crocheted Sweaters
Fair Isle Sweaters Simplified
Irresistible Knits
Knit It Your Way
Knitted Shawls, Stoles, and Scarves
Knitting with Novelty Yarns
Paintbox Knits
Simply Beautiful Sweaters
Simply Beautiful Sweaters for Men
The Ultimate Knitter's Guide

Our books are available at bookstores and your favorite craft, fabric and yarn retailers. If you don't see the title you're looking for, visit us at www.martingale-pub.com or contact us at:

1-800-426-3126

International: 1-425-483-3313

Fax: 1-425-486-7596

E-mail: info@martingale-pub.com

For more information and a full list of our titles, visit our Web site or call for a free catalog.